The Myth of Helter Skelter

Published by

Menelorelin Dorenay's Publishing

32742 Alipaz St. # 65
San Juan Capistrano, CA 92675
USA

© 2012

ISBN 978-0-9859832-1-5

The Myth of Helter Skelter

Susan Atkins-Whitehouse

Thank you from the editors to

Tony Hix,
Tracy Lamourie,
and David Madlala

for proof reading and input.

Special thanks from the editors to

Francis Zurcher

for endless citation work.

Table of Contents

Introduction by Susan		xi
Editor's Note		xv
1	The Slow, Easy Road to Disaster	1
2	The Bus Ride	5
3	The Error	19
4	First Appetite	25
5	The Hustle at Spahn Ranch	33
6	The House Fell	47
7	Running and Money	55
8	The Lie that Wouldn't Die	57
9	Black Riders	65
10	The Targeting of a Friend	67
11	The Killing of a Friend	71
12	The Tightening Trap	79
13	Selling Your Soul to Save Your Skin	83

14	A Desperate Plan	87
15	Into the Maelstrom	91
16	The Sickening Sigh of Relief	107
17	A New Desperation	111
18	Last Daylight	121
19	Pretrial Jail Time	123
20	The Pressure Inside	137
21	Being Thrown Away by Both Sides	151
22	The Selling of Bobby Beausoleil	163
23	And the Heavens Cried	169
24	The Lies that Bind	173
25	The Penalty Plan	175
26	Suicide on Command	183
27	The Difference Between Vampires and Angels	197
28	Life and Death Concurrently	215
29	Life After Death	221

Introduction by Susan

In the fall of 1986 I received a letter from a group of young people living in a commune in Colorado. There were about two dozen of them between the ages of eighteen and twenty-six and they wrote to tell me how "cool" they thought my commitment offense was. Apparently they failed to discover that I had disavowed Charles Manson over 15 years earlier.

I wrote them back explaining that nothing that happened back when I was with Charles Manson was "cool." Not the drug use, not the physical abuse, and certainly not the crimes. I suggested they find more enlightening role models and heroes.

Several weeks later I received their reply. It was an envelope with nothing inside but a photograph of them all holding up a huge banner with "f--- you" written across it.

Americans like their heroes to be Super Heroes and their villains to be Super Villains. It's part of our culture – a bigger-than-life country filled with bigger-than-life characters.

But real heroes are simply ordinary, fallible people who stand up for what they believe in even when they're scared, even when they're unsure of themselves, and even when no one is watching – they aren't made of steel. And criminals are simply fallible humans who make very bad decisions in their lives. They aren't anything worth admiring.

Over thirty-five years ago in Los Angeles, a crime took place which has been blown up to the point that it has attained mythological proportions in the minds of many people. The stories have become bigger and bigger until more people know the name of Charles Manson than that of Thurgood Marshall.

That is a tragedy.

This crime was not a devious, diabolical attempt to start Armageddon spawned by the mind of a Super Villain, nor was it a statement about environmental injustices. It was nothing more than an ugly, needless, senseless crime which destroyed families, hurt communities, and took irreplaceable loved ones out of the lives of those who needed them. It is neither amazing or interesting.

Unfortunately the fictionalization, exaggeration and media marketing of this crime and of the participants produces the very real risk of turning Charles Manson into a fictitious horror-movie character, or a comic-book villain nobody really believes in. And it produces the risk of making Charles Manson a hero to misguided young people who don't actually know anything about him. As thirty-five years come and go, in some circles it is actually debated whether Charles Manson participated in the crimes at all.

With this in mind it seems it is a good time to lay the crimes out the way I saw them back in 1969, and how I understand them now.

People are intrigued by what they don't understand and I think the "fantastic" nature of some of the reasons given for the crimes over the years has had the effect of making them a point of obsession. I believe if I can lay these crimes out so they are perfectly understandable, even boorishly so, maybe they will be seen as the horrific acts of brutality they were, and not as a tasteful point of interest or conversation among intelligent people.

With this in mind and as my impetus I feel it is time to produce the book you are about to read with me.

Susan Atkins-Whitehouse
2005

Editor's Note

Susan did not want to do this project. It wasn't fun for her. It wasn't fun for me either, but since I was representing her legally I thought it was important enough to try to put it together.

The District Attorneys who inherited the case from Vincent Bugliosi were, year by year, deliberately misrepresenting the facts and changing the story until it was almost entirely fiction. After September 11th, 2001 the District Attorneys literally started saying Manson's plan had been to help *Muslims overthrow the US government.* By 2009 they were literally calling it a "terrorist attack." In 2008 the District Attorneys looked the TV cameras and the parole board straight in the eye and insisted Susan had never helped the police and that she was responsible for *all* the wounds inflicted on Sharon Tate.

Thanks to the media this fiction was being turned into public reality. In 2009, when we forced the DA to admit that not only was Susan not responsible for all the wounds to Sharon Tate, but in fact the California Courts had determined there was no evidence to suggest Susan had ever stabbed Ms. Tate, all the newspapers continued to call Susan "the woman who killed Sharon Tate," with several even continuing to insist Susan was responsible for all Ms. Tate's wounds.

It was incredibly frustrating to discover that even when we read the Court decisions and the trial transcripts out in front of the TV cameras and showed them that the District Attorneys were lying to them, the media wouldn't even bother reporting it, but continued to simply repeat what the State told them to say.

The myth was becoming more important than the truth.

And so this was a last resort. And I'm guessing the people who fabricated the myth for their own agenda or enrichment will simply ignore this, but at least it's here for anyone who actually wants to try to see what really happened.

So we started this project with the understanding that any intelligent, objective reader would (should) naturally weigh Susan's uncorroborated account as suspect. It was also our hope that this book would be read by intelligent, objective readers.

With this in mind it was my intent to document and reference absolutely everything Susan said in order to produce what was hoped would be an account that is as objective as humanly possible.

An effort was made to limit the references and documentation to sources that were as credible as could be found. This means the primary source for reference was *Helter Skelter*, the account written and published by the Prosecutor Vincent Bugliosi himself. This account was written and published only a couple years after the events and according to Mr. Bugliosi it was taken from his notes made during the investigation and trial, which increases the chance it is not tainted by poor memory. Mr. Bugliosi defended the veracity of this account at least twice in court against civil suits. It was also produced by the very person who argued Susan should be executed. All of which makes this account the most convincing source for facts to support Susan's account.

There are also occasional references to the book written by Charles Watson, *Will You Die For Me?* This account was also produced about thirty years ago (copyrighted 1978), and so is less likely to contain unintentional memory errors. Like Susan's own account one might understandably question the truthfulness of Charles Watson's account, except to the extent he makes admissions against his own interest. (i.e. – it's hard to believe he would lie to make himself look worse.)

Further references are made to the book by Chaplain Ray, *God's Prison Gang*, in which Chaplain Ray interviewed both Susan and Charles Watson in 1975. Once again, while objective readers might question the truthfulness of statements made to exonerate themselves, it is hard to question statements made against their own self interest. It is also a good reference when challenging the continuing claims that

Susan has "changed her story" over the years. To this extent I feel this is a credible reference.

On occasion there are also references to things Manson himself told the writer of the book *Manson, In His Own Words*, which was published around 1980. (softbound version, ISBN 0-8021-3024-0) This account is, at points, wildly fictionalized and self serving. In all fairness, the biographer makes a point of stating Charles Manson appeared medicated to various degrees during the time he was being interviewed, so perhaps the fantastic parts of his story were not intentionally erroneous. In addition, a lot of his story seems prompted, which is to say it appears Manson is responding to questions concerning either Susan or Charles Watson's earlier published accounts, and not a direct account of his own memory. (It seems unlikely that, ten years after the fact, Charles Manson's memory of the crimes would touch on the very same several moments that Susan or Charles Watson's memory did.) While both of these facts make Charles Manson's account somewhat suspect, once again to the extent Manson makes statements against his own best interest it may once again be argued to be accurate - it is hard to see why he would lie to make himself look worse. So to this extent I have occasionally included citations to this work.

Lastly, there are occasional citations to Susan's own 1977 book, *Child of Satan, Child of God*. References to Susan's own book are not made with the purpose of convincing the reader as to their truthfulness, but simply to show this is the same account Susan gave 40 years ago. This is not "Susan's new version of the crimes."

This heavy footnoting may become ponderous at times, and we apologize for that. But this whole book is worthless if it is not a process toward a more thorough understanding of the events associated with this terrible tragedy, an undermining of the myth surrounding these events, and a means of producing an intelligent discussion of these events. Merely producing another unverifiable and wildly speculative account of these crimes serves no purpose at all other than to continue to hurt the families who have lost irreplaceable loved ones and to contribute to the aggrandizement of the myth of Charles Manson.

Tragedies like this shouldn't be discussed at all unless they are discussed with a legitimate goal. That goal should be to try to see that similar tragedies do not occur in the future.

James Whitehouse
2011

Chapter 1

The Slow, Easy Road to Disaster

At the age of thirteen my mother was diagnosed with inoperative cancer and I "inherited" a family of five. I would come home from junior high school and begin cooking, cleaning, and washing for my father, two brothers, myself and my bed-ridden mother. I was also the one who had to give my mother the morphine shots as she slowly passed away over the next twelve months. Upon her death my father increased his drinking until eventually, around my sixteenth birthday, he left one day and never came back, abandoning me and my younger brother to fend for ourselves.

By the age of nineteen I'd survived a series of nightmarish episodes to finally find a moment of stability among a group of people living in San Francisco in the counter-culture environment. At the time this was not a terrible place to be. Janis Joplin lived next-door. Mama Cass of The Mamas And The Papas taught me how to make BLT's. We were not "deviants," we were part of the artist subculture of the era.

That brief moment of stability ended when my friend Ella-Jo and I came home one day to find my place empty – my boyfriend had been arrested and once again I found myself completely broke and on my own. After three long years of fighting to survive and find some stability I was right back where I'd started. I didn't even have a place to sleep.

But Ella-Jo said it was okay, I could stay with her. And that's when I met a group of her friends who were all going down to Los Angeles for the summer. Ella-Jo said it ought to be great. She said I'd already met one of the guys — he had an old school bus and they were going to just pack it full of people and head off.

It sounded good. It was the summer of 1967. Young people were moving around and hitchhiking about the country. I'd been in San Francisco for a year or two and the prospect and starting over from nothing again didn't sound very compelling. How bad could a summer trip to L.A. be?

Hindsight is always perfect — I should have stayed in San Francisco.

The "guy with the old school bus" was, of course, Charles Manson. The story of how I got from the empty house in San Francisco to Death Row four years later is the single most personally painful story I know. I do not like remembering it, reflecting on it, or discussing it. Every year I receive numerous requests from media organizations, college students, law enforcement agencies, and inquisitive people asking for my story, or for explanations or reflections. Most these requests are tasteful. Most are sincere. Some are not. And every couple years the California Parole Board "invites" me to relive in detail the most horrible three days of my life.

It is only my firm conviction that talking about this now will serve the community that I am undertaking this painful and distasteful subject.

I think it is also important to show that big disasters do not start with a decision to create a disaster, but with a series of small poor decisions. No one wakes up one morning and decides they are going to run-amuck. One poor decision leads to a situation where you are forced to choose between two bad alternatives, and that decision in turn leads you deeper and deeper into a hole.

C.S. Lewis once said that the surest path to hell is the slow, easy descent with no sign-posts, no quick turns, no indication that anything is wrong.

This is as important a lesson out of this story as anything.

And so Ella-Jo and I set out on a light-hearted summer trip to L.A. with a group of young people.

The Myth of Helter Skelter

Chapter 2

The Bus Ride

The bus ride from San Francisco to Los Angeles took several months, moving through the trendy, counter-culture enclaves along the California coast. Communes and gurus were not uncommon in 1967. Religious sects and metaphysics were accepted and applauded. Teenagers were hitch-hiking across the country looking to "find" themselves, or to find some sort of spiritual enlightenment. One more bus load of truth-seekers was not even noticed.

Once we arrived in Los Angeles the journey to Spahn's Movie Ranch in Topanga took about a year as we bounced from one open house to another.

This period of time was relatively unimportant in the context of what was to follow except in a few notable ways.

First, this was the period when I got to know most of the people who ended up associated with the crimes. Bobby Beausoleil and his friends, including Leslie Van Houten and Catherine Share, joined the group. Patricia Krenwinkel was on the bus even before I arrived, as was Lenette Fromme. Sandra Good joined shortly afterwards.

And second, once we got to Spahn Ranch we were pretty well isolated from the rest of the world. Though it was just an hour's drive north of downtown Los Angeles this was an insurmountable distance if you didn't have a car. In the end this isolation made it much harder to avoid the insanity once it started, or to run even if one had the courage.

This is also the time when I got a better idea of who Charles Manson really was. Unfortunately I did not understand him well enough. I did not understand him the way I do today.

Making a Super Villain out of Charles Manson is a mistake. Claiming he is a criminal mastermind would actually be amusing if it wasn't at the price of so many lives.

Most of the attention the crimes have been given over the years has been generated by how "inexplicable" they were. Most people who show an interest do so merely because the motivation for the crimes seems so hard to fathom – people tend to attribute depth and intelligence to anything they can't understand.

In truth, these crimes were an incredible bungle — an incredible series of mistakes which, once tied together, started a chain reaction which sped on and on, faster and faster, unstoppably to a terrible conclusion.

If I do my job right, by the end of this book you will understand both these crimes and Charles Manson perfectly. There will be nothing that happened that won't make sense to you. You will understand Charles Manson and the crimes in a way the prosecuting attorney for the case, Vincent Bugliosi, never truly did. You will understand Charles Manson in a way that, unfortunately, few of the young people at Spahn Ranch in the fall of 1969 understood him. And you will understand him in a way that took me losing my freedom and thirty-six years of my life to understand him.

The two and a half years I had the misfortune to live around Charles Manson was longer than almost any of the people who stayed with him. Unlike most of the young people moving about the country in the late 1960's, I didn't have a family to go back to. Unlike the prodigal son, I couldn't hitch hike across the country, sow my wild oats, express my youthful rebelliousness, and return home when I became tired and disillusioned. By the time I realized what was happening I was stuck.[1]

---

[1] "For Susan, I realized, the Family was her only family." [Vincent Bugliosi] (*Helter Skelter*, pg. 255)

But it means I was there to see the entire thing develop. I was there to see why it happened. So this story comes from someone who saw more of Charles Manson than most the people he associated with, someone who told the police Charles Manson was responsible for the crimes, and someone who has spent the last thirty-six years avoiding his disciples, ignoring his threats, and burning his hate-mail. In short, I found out more about Charles Manson than anyone would want to, and in the hardest way.

Maybe this book will allow some of you to avoid repeating my mistakes.

Perhaps the best place to start is with a better understanding of Charles Manson himself.

There is a tendency to simply assume that people in prison for murder are murderers because there is something in them that isn't like the rest of us. That's a very reassuring notion – it sets a very clear line between us and the people we think of as "bad." The problem is that you end up believing people who kill do so because they're murderers on the inside, and the proof they are murderers on the inside is the fact that they killed someone. This doesn't leave any real room for intelligent understanding of the factors that lead to crime.

The real question is what led to these crimes. What led to so many horrifically bad decisions? Why were these crimes orchestrated? What did anyone hope to gain from them?

Prosecutor Vincent Bugliosi stated that there is no such thing as a motiveless crime – it is an animal that doesn't exist.[2]

I believe this is true.

Psychologists sometimes speak of sociopaths. Sociopaths, if they really exist, could be explained as people who don't understand that other people are *people*. That is to say they don't really understand on an emotional level that you and I have the same needs and wants that they do. They may understand that you and I are people on an intellectual level – in fact that is usually the source of a great deal of their ability to manipulate others – but this intellectual understanding doesn't effect them. Most of us couldn't steal candy from a baby. Most of us couldn't call someone up and tell them their child had been harmed. We understand what an emotional trauma that would be and we associate with it so closely that it would cause us incredible emotional pain to put another person through that. According to psychologists a sociopath wouldn't make that association. He would understand that people would get upset about their child being harmed, but he wouldn't identify with the emotional pain at all. This means a sociopath would be able to

---

[2] "Occasionally writers refer to "motiveless crimes." I've never encountered such an animal, and I'm convinced that none such exists." (*Helter Skelter*, pg. 184)

be incredibly manipulative because he wouldn't feel any remorse about hurting people.

Charles Manson may be a sociopath. Or he may simply be someone who was so badly abused growing up that he had to learn to turn off that part of himself. Perhaps his emotional responses were beaten out of him. Or perhaps excessive use of drugs led to paranoia which caused him to develop imaginary enemies who were trying to harm him, blunting any human sympathy he might have had for them.

Psychologists still argue over how to separate true sociopaths – those who truly don't have a concept of other people as anything other than objects – and those who simply no longer care about the needs and rights of others. There is a tendency to say that anyone who does a heinous crime is a sociopath because they obviously had no feelings for the hopes and dreams of their victims, but this is a mistake.

Almost always you will find that these are people who were hardened and embittered to the point they no longer cared about anything – not even their own life. But they still had a concept of other people as human beings.

Considerable media attention has been given to Charles Manson's ability to "control the minds of his followers." His ability to "brainwash" people. "Hypnotize." "Zombyize." But if you look at his methods of controlling people you will see no mystic clairvoyance, no unearthly super-power. What you will see is that he knows no more about brainwashing than any other pimp in Los Angeles.

He took young people, primarily girls, who had poor family relations, low self-esteem, and who felt they didn't belong. He took them away from all their familiar surroundings. He took them to an isolated place where he could control what they saw, heard, and learned.[3] He prevented them from making any attachments outside his group. He took away all their money under the pretext that the Family would provide for them – which not only prevented them from leaving but also made them dependent on him *even for their clothes, food and shelter*. He sowed dissension and bitterness toward outsiders. He encouraged them to become dependent on drugs – drugs which he alone would disperse.[4] And then, to polish it all off, he threw in a sizable portion of brutal physical abuse.[5, 6]

---

[3] "As Manson himself once remarked in court: "You can convince anybody of anything if you just push it at them all of the time. They may not believe it 100 percent, but they will still draw opinions from it, especially if they have no other information to draw their opinions from." Therein lies another of the keys he used: in addition to repetition, he used isolation." (*Helter Skelter*, pg. 654 & 655)

[4] "...grass, Peyote, LSD, whatever was available -- Manson rationing them out, deciding how much each person needed. "Everything was done at Charlie's direction," Paul [Watkins] said."(*Helter Skelter*, pg. 318)

[5] "Once a pimp acquires a girl who is willing to work as a whore, he must have three qualities to hold on to her. All three

I think most people would be surprised to learn that Charles Manson's "brainwashing" often took the form of beating a teenage girl to the point she was bloodied and screaming when she didn't do what he wanted. Diane Lake was fourteen when thirty-five-year-old Manson broke a chair over her head for talking when she wasn't supposed to.[7] When Mary Brunner tried to take her son away from the Family she was beaten so badly she couldn't get out of bed for three days.

Often, Charles Manson's "mind control" took an even crueler turn. When Linda Kasabian wanted to leave Spahn Ranch after the Cielo and LaBianca murders, her daughter was moved away from the

---

actually amount to maintaining some kind of respect, the nature of the girl establishing the procedure the pimp must use. Fear and intimidation control most prostitutes..." (*Manson, in His Own Words*, pg. 92)

[6] "...Still, through the drugs and listening to the ways a particular leader or guru maneuvered his people, some of their rap may have become embedded in my subconscious. Planting fear in their people is the way a lot of leaders keep control. At the time, love and doing our own thing was what held us together and that's the way I wanted everything to be, but at a later date, the things I was exposed to... may have come back to me." (*Manson, in His Own Words*, pg. 123)

[7] "Apparently not finding Dianne [Lake] submissive enough, Manson had, on various occasions: punched her in the mouth; kicked her across the room; hit her over the head with a chair leg; and whipped her with an electrical cord." (*Helter Skelter*, pg. 275)

The Bus Ride

ranch to a secluded place surrounded by armed thugs. Charles Manson claimed the children were being "protected" but in reality the they were being held as security to prevent their mothers from leaving — the obvious message was that Charles Manson was in complete control of the children's lives.[8, 9, 10] This is the same type of "persuasion" which helped contribute to my decision to recant my Grand Jury testimony and "confess" that Charles Manson had nothing to do with the murders – Charles Manson sent his followers to suggest that it might be better for me and my son if I decided not to testify against him.[11, 12]

---

[8] "...The mothers were not allowed to care for their own children. They separated her [Kasabian] and Tanya [her daughter, two years old]..." (*Helter Skelter*, pg. 349)

[9] "Her [Kasabian's] testimony was also at times very moving. Telling How Manson separated the Mothers and their children, and relating her own feelings on being parted from Tanya, Linda said, "Sometimes, you know, when there wasn't anybody around, especially Charlie, I would give her my love and feed her." (*Helter Skelter*, pg. 434)

[10] "Linda told me [Bugliosi] that she decided to flee after the night of the LaBianca murders; however, Manson sent her to the waterfall area later that day (August 11) and she was afraid to leave that night because of the armed guards he had posted." (*Helter Skelter*, pg. 389)

[11] "Since the birth of my [Susan's] baby, Charlie had an additional grip on me to go along with my addiction to his internal power, which I thought was from God. If I got out of line, Charlie would subtly maneuver me to the children and go to work on me about their security and future. He frequently became cruel, manifest most horribly when he would take my

This type of cruelty has nothing to do with "mind control." It takes no special powers to threaten and brutalize teenagers and young adults. This is not a very impressive achievement and Charles Manson deserves no awe or respect for it. Such brutality does, however, take a special *type* of person.[13]

And Charles Manson was a social person, he is not a loner or an isolationist. He has to have people around him.[14] Such a need is sometimes the sign of someone extremely insecure about themself. It can also be the sign of someone with extremely low self-esteem. Both are probably true for Charles Manson. His insecurity probably shows through in his belief

---

baby by the feet and swing him around and around high over his head and then down to within an inch of the rocky ground. He was crazy at those moments." (*Child of Satan, Child of God*, pg. 115)

[12] [Editor's Note: At Susan's 2005 parole hearing the Board read a letter sent to them from Barbara Hoyt who told them how Susan wasn't allowed to see her son, although Hoyt seemed to remember that Linda Kasabian was.]

[13] "I [Bugliosi] would learn, from talking to other Family members, that Manson would seek out each individual's greatest fear – not so the person could confront and eliminate it, but so he could re-emphasize it. It was like a magic button, which he could push at will to control that person." (*Helter Skelter*, pg. 321)

[14] MANSON: "...I was a long way from being a recluse, for certain parts of my make up demand I have someone around me..." (*Manson, in His Own Words*, pg. 137)

that he had to mirror back at people what he thought they wanted to see.[15] His low self-esteem probably shows through in his need to degrade, brutalize, and control weaker people around him.

Charles Manson is also a con-man. He will constantly try to get you to underestimate him. He will try to make you feel sorry for him. He will tell you how bad life has been to him, and how rough his upbringing was. That his mother didn't want him. That his teachers were mean to him. That society withdrew from him. He will tell you that fate itself and nothing else pushed him to the place he is now. But this is just a learned con – it is not true.

Charles Manson had everything. At one time he had almost twenty young girls taking care of him. He hobnobbed with the Beach Boys and attended Hollywood parties with musicians and movie stars. He lived for free off the generosity of soft-hearted people who believed in him — like Dennis Wilson of the Beach Boys — and off the hard work of the young girls who took him in. He never once had a job in the three years he was out of jail. Free drugs. Free sex. Famous people around him. He lived a dream life. He was offered everything America could offer a single man in the late 1960's. And he had it in the most hedonistic city in the country – Los Angeles.

---

[15] "Manson --a mirror which reflected the desires of others." (*Helter Skelter*, pg. 438)

The Myth of Helter Skelter

Society gave Charles Manson *so many* opportunities to make good. Hollywood forgave his sexual debauchery with under-age girls. Los Angeles forgave his drug use. The music industry and the counter-culture overlooked his prison time. Charles Manson was finally rejected by society not, as he likes to tell it, because they were cruel and worldly establishment people who didn't want to "get off his back." Charles Manson was finally rejected by society because he was a manipulative USER who abused the people who tried to be nice to him.

Everyone who ever tried to help Charles Manson was ultimately made a fool for their troubles. Dennis Wilson, who claimed to have spent as much as $100,000 on Manson, was threatened with the death of his son when he finally cut the money off.[16] Terry Melcher, who had tried to sell Manson's music to the industry, was targeted for murder when none of the offers came through.[17] Gary Hinman, who had

---

[16] "Dennis [Wilson] told me [Bugliosi] that he didn't have any trouble with Charlie until August of 1969 – Dennis could not recall the exact date, but he did know it was after the Tate murders – when Manson visited him, demanding $1,500 so he could go to the desert. When Wilson refused, Charlie told him, "Don't be surprised if you never see your kid again." Dennis had a seven-year-old son, and obviously this was one reason for his reluctance to testify." (*Helter Skelter*, pg. 340)

[17] "Of all the prosecution witnesses, Melcher was the most frightened of Manson. His fear was so great, he told me that he had been under psychiatric treatment and had employed a full-time bodyguard since December 1969 [almost a year earlier]. ...

donated food and clothing to feed and clothe Manson's own baby son, was murdered when he wouldn't give Manson money. Sandra Good's father helped support Charles Manson after his daughter joined the Family and was threatened when he wouldn't give more.[18]

And perhaps cruelest of all (save only the murder of Gary Hinman), a whole group of young people who looked up to and trusted Manson as a leader and guide were ultimately mislead, used, and then either thrown away or left to die. I don't speak so much for myself but for the younger kids at the ranch back in 1969. The young runaways who, thanks to Charles Manson, were fed a mouthful of bitterness toward the law and society and then pulled into auto theft, drug dealing, stealing, burglarizing, and for some a life of crime and addictions they would never overcome.

So if Charles Manson had it tough it was his own doing. Life gave him everything and he spit it back in society's face.

Melcher was so nervous, however, that he had to be given a tranquilizer before taking the stand." (*Helter Skelter*, pg. 510-511)

[18] "...Sandra Good, for example, claimed that her father, a San Diego stockbroker, had disowned her, neglecting to mention that this was only after he had sent her thousands of dollars and was threatened by Manson if he didn't give her more." (*Helter Skelter*, pg. 569)

In hindsight I've come to believe the most prominent character trait Charles Manson displays is that of a Manipulator. Not a guru, not a metaphysic, not a philosopher, not an environmentalist, not a sociologist or social activist, and not even a murderer. His long-term behavior is one predominantly of a practiced Manipulator.[19]

But this analysis is all from an intellectual level, and it has taken me years and years to be able to see Charles Manson like this. On an emotional level I could have told you about Charles Manson thirty-six years ago – he is a liar, a con artist, a physical abuser of women and children, a psychological and emotional abuser of human beings, a thief, a dope pusher, a kidnapper, a child stealer, a pimp, a rapist, and a child molester. I can attest to all of these things with my own eyes. And he was all of these things *before* he was a murderer[20].

---

[19] "Manson had a talent for sensing, and capitalizing on, a person's hangups and/or desires." (*Helter Skelter*, pg. 317)

[20] "One thirteen-year-old girls's initiation into the Family consisted of her being sodomized by Manson while others watched. Manson also "went down on" a young boy to show the others he had rid himself of all inhibitions." (*Helter Skelter*, pg. 319)

Chapter 3

The Error

So how did the Prosecutor, Vincent Bugliosi, make the mistake of concluding that Helter Skelter — a black/white race war that would bring on Armageddon — was the motive for the murders of the LaBiancas and those at 10050 Cielo Drive?

The most obvious reason is that Mr. Bugliosi didn't look at the events that led up to these murders in chronological order. If you don't study what happened in the order it happened how can you ever understand why one occurrence followed another?

Did Charles Manson simply wake up one morning and say, 'Somebody's going to die today'? Mr. Bugliosi gives that impression in his version of the crime. What Mr. Bugliosi doesn't answer satisfactorily is *why* it happened. Mr. Bugliosi says the murders were planned to bring about Helter Skelter but Vincent Bugliosi also claimed that Charles Manson already believed Helter Skelter was imminent.[21] So, why would he risk his life to try to set it off himself?

Charles Manson went to a great deal of trouble to avoid responsibility for the murders. He tried to get others to do the killing for him, he tried to distance himself from the places where the murders took place, he ran to the desert, he set up alibis, he set up armed guards around himself and his camp.[22] He did not want to be caught. And it wasn't that he didn't understand the consequences of his actions. He knew very well what would happen if he was caught.

So, if Helter Skelter was already imminent why did he take such terrible risks? It just doesn't make sense. And when things don't make sense it generally means you haven't got the story quite right.

If Charles Manson thought Helter Skelter was imminent, and if his elaborate efforts indicated just how desperately he didn't want to get caught, why would he still go ahead and arrange for people to be murdered?

---

[21] "Charles Manson was already talking about an imminent black-white war when Gregg Jakobson first met him, in the spring of 1968. There was an underground expression current at the time, "the shit is coming down," variously interpreted as meaning the day of judgment was at hand or all hell was breaking loose..." (*Helter Skelter*, pg. 329)

[22] "At night everyone was required to wear dark clothing, so as to be less conspicuous, and eventually Manson posted armed guards, who roamed the ranch until dawn." (*Helter Skelter*, pg. 349)

He wouldn't.

Something else provoked this rash act. And as we go through the events that led to those two nights in August 1969, you will begin to see exactly how a long line of interrelated events produced this crime. And only then will you begin to understand the true tragedy of the horrible loss of life that ensued.

But for now it is worth pointing out, in Mr. Bugliosi's defense, that the Tate-LaBianca trial was rushed from the start due to the incredible amount of public pressure the Los Angeles Police Department was under. The Grand Jury was held before the District Attorney's Office had any real evidence on *anyone* except for my testimony. Because of this Mr. Bugliosi was forced into the case much quicker than he would have liked. He had to come up with a way to convict Charles Manson of crimes which Mr. Bugliosi knew he was responsible for but for which Charles Manson had been very careful to distance himself from.

This began what might be called the hunt for the Magic Motive.[23] That is to say 'the hunt for anything that would convince a jury that Charles Manson, and Charles Manson alone, was the beneficiary of these murders.'

---

[23] "*Why?* The biggest and most puzzling question of all remained "what was Manson's motive?" ...[After checking the horoscopes] It was indicative of our desperation that I went to such unlikely lengths in trying to ascertain why Manson had ordered these murders." (*Helter Skelter*, pg. 263)

In his book Mr. Bugliosi points out that the motive is not the prosecuting attorney's job to establish. But this case was different. If no motive was established there would be no way of convicting Charles Manson. And so Mr. Bugliosi jumped in as any young, ambitious attorney would have and began digging around. But he didn't find out that the murder of Gary Hinman was connected to Bernard Crowe until well after the Grand Jury. How could he possibly uncover the real motive for the murders of those at the Cielo and LaBianca homes without understanding the real reason for Gary Hinman's death?

He couldn't.

It wasn't until the trial started that Vincent Bugliosi finally found out about the suspected murder of Bernard Crowe.[24] This suspected murder would have an incredible effect on the actions of Charles Manson, but by the time Vincent Bugliosi discovered it he was already selling Helter Skelter to a jury. To have tried to change the purported motive at that point would have cost him his credibility in a case in which he was already stretching his credibility to the limit.

---

[24] [Editor's Note: Bernard Crowe was not murdered, but Charles Manson did not know this until after the beginning of the trial. Everything that was done during the last five months of 1969 was done with the belief that Bernard Crowe had been killed and that he was a member of the black militant group the Black Panthers.]

So Vincent Bugliosi went on with Helter Skelter. To his credit, and a testament to his hard work, he won convictions and death sentences. But this misrepresentation of the motive has had some disturbing side-effects. The most disturbing, as far as I am concerned, is the raising of Charles Manson to the status of a mystic, mind-controlling Super Villain. The attention he has received as a result of his conviction is not what is deserved.

The second disturbing side-effect of the Helter Skelter myth is that it allows several of those who were involved with Charles Manson at the time of the murders, and a whole new generation of misguided youth, to delude themselves as to what these murders were really about.

They were not revolutionary or environmental symbolic killings. They were the completely unnecessary murders of innocent people — people with loved ones, families, friends, dreams and hopes just like the rest of us — and all for the basest and most arrogant of causes; the serving of Charles Manson's self-interest.

The Myth of Helter Skelter

Chapter 4

First Appetite

By the fall of 1969, Charles Manson had as many as 40 people living with him at Spahn Ranch.

I often hear it asked, why did people flock to this obviously abusive and oppressive deviant? Why did those who stayed feel drawn to his murder-cult? How could those involved with Charles Manson deliberately draw more people into his nightmarish web of fear and hatred?

These are the types of questions you hear posed by those who look back from a point in time *after* 1970. For them it seems impossible to believe that the commune wasn't steeped in murder and revolution from the start, but it wasn't. Without knowing the whole story of what led up to the murders in the fall of 1969, it's very easy to doubt that an ordinary hippie commune, preaching love and music and drugs, could be transformed into what the Family became. It's very easy, without knowing what happened, to insist the

Family must always have been a dark, bitter, twisted and homicidal group. But that's not true.[25]

The Family started as something very different and then it changed. It was only over a relatively short period of time that it became what the media shows you today. But to understand this long road you must understand how it began.

In 1967, Charles Manson was released into Los Angeles after spending the last seven years of his life in federal prison. His interests upon leaving prison were few – sex and drugs. The day after his release he transferred his parole to San Francisco, where the new hippie movement and 'free love' promised both.

Charles Manson must have been in heaven once he was turned loose in San Francisco. Years of learning how to manipulate and con, as well as years of studying pseudo-religions, paid off in spades. San Francisco was filled with young, naive, idealistic and impressionable kids just looking for someone to show them a new way. And they were willing to throw themselves into any new experience or idea whole-heartedly, forsaking everything else.

In 1967, Charles Manson could talk new-age religion. Charles Manson could talk old religion.

---

[25] [Editor's Note: Susan never used the term "the Family" and she finds it offensive. This is a term coined by Charles Manson and then adopted by the Prosecutor. It is used here simply because it has become part of the cultural vernacular, and it is convenient.]

Charles Manson knew eastern religious thought. Charles Manson had the vision and intensity necessary to hold the attention of young minds. He understood psychology. He understood nihilism. He gave the appearance of having forsaken his worldly possessions and dropped out of the rat-race (in truth, this appearance was simply because he left prison with very little and even less to give up). He appeared to live what he preached.

And what did Charles Manson want? What was he after? Sex and drugs. But these were available everywhere in the hippie counter-culture – they were practically given away. So Charles Manson strung together a little pseudo-religious pseudo-intellectual mumbo-jumbo, along with his ability to play guitar, and he was in. The thirty-five year old con-man became a peace-loving hippie and began hanging around the parks and universities. And he used this new 'con' to get what he wanted.

So why did young people flock around him? Because in 1967, pseudo-spiritual sermons with a vaguely eastern feel to them were what people wanted to hear. And Charles Manson was an expert at telling people what they wanted to hear. Years of learning how to mimic and ingratiate himself to other inmates in prison had taught him how to draw out people's opinions and attitudes and project these back at them.

Why weren't these young people able to see through his 'con'? Because drugs and sex were things that were shared casually in the underground. Nobody

The Myth of Helter Skelter

but Charles Manson would have perceived these things as something you had to cheat people out of.

So, when people ask how members of the Family could ever have been attracted to Charles Manson the true answer often shocks and offends them – in 1967, there was no reason to fear Charles Manson. He wasn't preaching murder, he was preaching love and peace (not out of any belief in these things necessarily, but as a way of getting what he wanted). There was no reason to avoid Charles Manson in 1967.[26]

People often ask why members of the Family stayed with Charles Manson. Once again, the answer is often received with incredible disbelief – until the summer of 1969, there was no reason to run from Charles Manson. He could get what he wanted by playing the part of the pacifist hippie guru. No one suspected that this facade hid an all encompassing and violently dangerous self interest.

And, yes, if *you* had been searching for something in San Francisco or Los Angeles in the late 60's, and you had run into Charles Manson, he would have told you whatever it was that you wanted to hear and you would have been taken in. You would have thought he was a great guy. You would have thought

---

[26] " "Before Helter Skelter came along," Watkins said with a sigh of wistful nostalgia, "all Charlie cared about was orgies." " (*Helter Skelter*, pg. 331)

he shared your beliefs and your understanding of the world, and you'd have thought you could trust him.

If you were searching for something in San Francisco or Los Angeles (or anywhere up and down the West Coast), as many of us were in those times, and you *did not* end up with Charles Manson it was only by God's good grace and not by any better judgment of your own.

But it's hard for people to believe this.

And I understand that. It's very frightening to accept that if you had been there something like the Family could have grown up right around you without your having any forewarning. It is much more comforting to believe that something this horrible could not have been born without the knowledge and participation of those around. It is much more comforting to believe there must have been obvious signs from the beginning – there must have been some reason this did *not* begin just like every other commune experimenting with drugs and free sex at the time.

It is frightening to believe that, but for the love of God, you weren't pulled into that nightmare as well. It is much more appealing to convince yourself that those who ended up there were somehow different from the rest of the young kids on the West Coast in the late 60's. That somehow they must have been intrinsically evil to end up where they did. That they had a taste for Charles Manson's bitter preachings.

That you would have avoided Charles Manson. That you would have seen through his cons.

But you wouldn't have. [27]

In 1967, Charles Manson's needs and interests were so nominal he didn't seem any more manipulative or dangerous than the boy next door – all he wanted was a little sex and drugs. There were no 'bitter preachings' about hate and killing and 'pigs.' There was no need. Charles Manson could get all he wanted by copying and mirroring the love and peace rhetoric of the day. And he did it well. His years as a pimp and a con man had taught him to say what people around him wanted to hear, and to say it convincingly.

Very few people who met Charles Manson during this period weren't attracted to him. Even his parole officer, who was familiar with ex-convicts and their manipulations, was taken in by Manson.[28] Most

---

[27] "I have never commented on your case, as I was not happy with the media circus that has always exploited it. I have been particularly unhappy with Mr. Bugliosi's distorted use of my professional testimony - to argue against your release. I testified that anyone's children could have ended up in your situation as part of a shared psychosis. He has repeatedly stated that I said just the opposite…" (Dr. Joel Hochman, 2009, Psychiatrist for the prosecution at the trial)

[28] " "There are a lot of Charlies running around, believe me," observed Roger Smith, Manson's parole officer during his San Francisco period." (*Helter Skelter*, pg. 222)

of those who heard Charles Manson speak stayed with him. Those who escaped the nightmare to come did so not due to their better judgment, but because they were lucky enough to be left behind when the Family moved from place to place.

I, unfortunately, was not one of those who was left behind.

The Myth of Helter Skelter

Chapter 5

The Hustle at Spahn Ranch

The movement of the Family to Los Angeles was the beginning of Charles Manson's manipulation, no longer just for sex and drugs, but for control of the people around him. Having satiated himself with the fruits of the free love counter-culture that had been denied him for so long while in prison, his goals were raised. He now wanted more.

This is also the point in the story when I personally become involved.

A pimp has to know how to control people. Especially women. Especially young women. Absolute control is essential if you want to make someone do something that is personally repugnant to them.

The first rule of controlling people to this extent is to remove the people you want to manipulate from all familiar surroundings and support. This not only makes them dependent on the you for everything, it means if they begin to have misgivings there is nowhere to turn. And there is no one around to reinforce their own inner feeling that things aren't the way they should be.[29, 30]

Charles Manson knew this. Not only is this a basic manipulative tool, he'd had practice. He'd been a pimp at one time in his checkered past.

Once he settled at Spahn Ranch in Los Angeles, Charles Manson's wants and needs reached even higher. He had men to get him money and drugs and to do his dirty work. He had women for sex and to take care of him. But this wasn't enough. He'd seen the fruits of fame. He wanted power. He now sought social acceptance.

The story of his ill-fated music career is not a unique one. Only one in a thousand make it in music

---

[29] "Once a pimp acquires a girl who is willing to work as a whore, he must have three qualities to hold on to her. All three actually amount to maintaining some kind of respect, the nature of the girl establishing the procedure the pimp must use. Fear and intimidation control most prostitutes..." (*Manson, in His Own Words*, pg. 92)

[30] "Manson himself once remarked in court: "You can convince anybody of anything if you just push it at them all of the time. They may not believe it 100 percent, but they will still draw opinions from it, especially if they have no other information to draw their opinions from." ...Therein lies still another of the keys he used: in addition to repetition, he used isolation. There were no newspapers at Spahn Ranch, no clocks. Cut off from the rest of society, he created in this timeless land a tight little society of his own, with its own value system. It was holistic, complete, and totally at odds with the world outside." (*Helter Skelter*, pg. 655)

– maybe less. But this was an incredible blow to a man who actually thought he was the only thing that mattered in the universe. The piquing of his pride can only be imagined.

But Manson's brush with fame – the Beach Boys and the Hollywood crowd – drew even more people to Charles Manson's Family during this time. And there was still no reason for them not to be drawn in. It was basically the same sermon he had been using in San Francisco, only there were more kids and fewer counter-culture gurus to compete with in Los Angeles. Charles Manson became better at telling his stories, learning what best held the interests and imaginations of the idealistic youths. And as the Family grew a hierarchy developed. Those who pleased Charles Manson more were given preferential treatment, thus allowing him to increase his control over them.

But this was probably no different from any other commune based on a single leader. Some move closer to him and therefore benefit from increased acceptance, others find themselves on the outside and so work harder to get back in.

This might be a good point in the story to explain that *I* was never "on the inside." I was always an outsider. Because of my abusive upbringing I had a natural aversion to authority, and ironically even though Charles Manson preached against societal authority the more he took control of the Family the more he *became* the authority. Charles Manson and I always had a personality clash. I didn't like being told what to do and he demanded that people did what he told them.

At the time I thought that meant he was strong – I thought it meant he couldn't be dissuaded from his beliefs. He said he liked me and I thought he did, but when I wanted something he never gave it to me. Other men I'd known always tried to give me whatever I wanted in relationships – Charles Manson didn't. In hindsight I now understand it simply meant he didn't care in the least for anyone's interests except his own. He told me he liked me simply because that was a way to control me, a way to get me to contribute to the Family. Two years later, during the trial, when he made me and my co-defendants get on the stand and say that *we* planned the murders in a bid to allow him to escape the death penalty, thereby assuring our own executions, I discovered just how much he really cared about me.

One would expect to find great clues to the turning of the Family during this period, as this is the year or so that directly preceded the crimes. But there were no obvious signs that things were changing from the peace and love sermons in San Francisco. There were clues, but they were very subtle.

The influx of new Family members was one of these changes. It was nothing alarming of itself, but it did mean that a group mentality was forming. It also meant it was easier to pretend everything that happened among us was all right – there was reassurance in numbers. Also, the slow decline into crime would eventually be cushioned and anesthetized by the fact that everyone around you was participating, so it didn't seem out of the ordinary.

The development of the hierarchy was another.

The hierarchy was a little more profound. It changed Charles Manson from simply a new-age spiritual leader to the person who influenced everything that was done around Spahn Ranch. From the clothes you wore to the way you wore your hair, the merest comment from Manson sent people scurrying to please him. In the end it was his ability to simply do no more than "suggest" something be done to make it happen that lead to his erroneous belief that he couldn't be held responsible for the crimes.

He was wrong.

But at the beginning the change was slow and the effect was not yet obvious in late 1968 and early 1969.

Another change was the beginning of revolutionary talk. This was the beginning of the talk of Helter Skelter. The notion of a black/white race war was, of course, something Charles Manson had picked up in prison. That it began to come out more and more often was an indicator of the things being said by the young people who began joining the

The Myth of Helter Skelter

Family during this time. A consummate manipulator, Charles Manson simply parroted back at people what they most wanted to hear.[31] With the Watts riots in Los Angeles in 1965, and the growing fervor over Viet Nam, revolution was a popular catch-phrase for snaring the young, the idealistic, and the unwanted. And so Charles Manson sewed together several disjointed ideas and began to construct a tale so incredible and fanciful that it could hold the attention of even the most drug-enfeebled teenage mind. And the story of Helter Skelter was born.

That Charles Manson's Helter Skelter story was around will not be disputed. That he used it to manipulate the young people around him is abundantly obvious. But the contention that this had any relation to the true motive for the murders will slowly become ridiculous as the events are unfolded.

In his new quest for power, Charles Manson went out of his way to ensnare the lost and unwanted young. This is another indicator of his expertise in manipulation. They were the easiest to control. They had no one else to turn to. He, being an unwanted child himself, knew how to play on their inner bitterness and fear and longing to be accepted. But this might also be an over-simplification. Charles

---

[31] "That Manson foresaw a war between the blacks and the whites was not fantastic. Many people believe that such a war may someday occur." (*Helter Skelter*, pg. 293)

Manson tried to snare anyone he could. That he was more successful with the outcasts among society probably had little to do with his choice and more to do with the fact that outcasts had few other options open to them.

As an example, by the time of the crimes I had no family or friends left to turn to. My mother had passed away when I was fourteen, my father had abandoned my brother and me and gone off drinking when I was sixteen, my Aunt kicked me out of her house when I was eighteen because she caught my cousin drinking and was positive I was responsible, and my grandparents wouldn't speak to me after I had a child out of wedlock. Any friends I had before moving to Los Angeles were lost. Any friends I made in Los Angeles were harassed by the Family until they either joined or were scared away.

By 1969, I had nowhere in the world to go outside of Spahn Ranch.[32, 33] If I had left in early 1969, I would have left with my son and no friends, no family, no money, no food, and literally only the clothes I was wearing. By late 1969, even this meager

---

[32] "Her mother had died of cancer while Susan was still in her teens, and, after numerous quarrels with her father, she'd dropped out of high school and drifted to San Francisco. ...I had a certain amount of pity for her." (*Helter Skelter*, pg. 229)

[33] "For Susan, I realized, the Family was her only family." (*Helter Skelter*, pg. 255)

The Myth of Helter Skelter

chance would be eliminated and those who left were lucky to leave with their lives.[34]

Probably the most important change in the Family that took place during the year or so before the murders is also the least mentioned. That is the increase in drug use.

Drug use tends to produce an ever increasing appetite. Once you start you slowly become conditioned to them and you need progressively more and more drugs to feel the high you did the first time you tried them. This is a very subtle thing and in 1968 it was not much cause for alarm, but Charles Manson was becoming hooked.

His initial interest in a career in music faded in part because of the spurn he felt he received from the music industry, but also because his wants were changing. The Family was growing daily in Los Angeles. Arriving with only seven members, by the time he settled at Spahn Ranch the Family sometimes

---

[34] "On the night of October 9... At about 4 A.M. as several of the officers [in the first Barker raid] were proceeding down one of the draws some distance from the ranch, they spotted two males asleep on the ground. Between them was a sawed-off shotgun. The two, Clem Tufts [t/n Steve Grogan] and Randy Morglea [t/n Hugh Rocky Todd], were placed under arrest. Though the officers were unaware of it, the pair had been stalking human game: Stephanie Schram and Kitty Lutesinger, two seventeen-year-old girls who fled the ranch the previous day." (*Helter Skelter*, pg. 170)

reached up to as many as forty people, counting the hangers on.[35] Just providing enough food became a project – you can imagine what the expenses for drugs were. And for Charles Manson this became a very important consideration.

By the summer of 1969, most expenses at Spahn Ranch were financed by drug deals and auto theft. All activity around Charles Manson and the men he trusted concerned procuring drugs or money for drugs. Drugs had been one of Charles Manson's primary tools for manipulating people ever since blending into the San Francisco underground, but now I believe *they* had a hold of *him*.

The extent to which this is true can be seen in accounts of life at Spahn Ranch during this time. Sandra Good was reported to have given Charles Manson thousands of dollars upon joining the Family.[36] Linda Kasabian confessed to stealing

---

[35] "This was our initial estimate of the size of the Family. We'd later learn that at various times it numbered a hundred or more. The hard-core members – i.e. those who remained for any length of time and who were privy to what was going on – numbered between twenty-five and thirty." (*Helter Skelter*, pg. 200)

[36] "Sandra Good, for example, claimed that her father, a San Diego stockbroker, had disowned her, neglecting to mention that this was only after he had sent her thousands of dollars and was threatened by Manson if he didn't give her more." (*Helter Skelter*, pg. 569)

$5,000 and giving it to the Family.[37] Juanita donated over $10,000 and her van, turning it all over to Charles Manson.[38] And poor Dennis Wilson estimated he spent close to $100,000 on Charles Manson during the several months he provided for the Family.[39, 40] And where did this money go? The

---

[37] "...Charles Melton, the hippie philanthropist from whom Linda had stolen the $5,000." (*Helter Skelter*, pg. 392)

[38] "...T.J. [Wallemen], Clem [Grogan], Tex [Watson], and Ella were hitchhiking back to the ranch. They were picked up by a girl named Juanita driving a new travel van and by the time they arrived back at Spahn, they had Juanita convinced she should spend some time with us. Juanita dug our lifestyle and jumped right in on all our activities. The van became ours and in addition, she contributed over ten thousand dollars to our needs." (*Manson, in His Own Words*, pg. 152)

[39] "They [the Family] stayed for several months [at Dennis Wilson's house], during which time the group more than doubled in number. ... The experience, Dennis later estimated cost him about $100,000. Besides Manson's constantly hitting him for money, Clem [Grogan] demolished Wilson's uninsured $21,000 Mercedes-Benz by plowing it into a mountain on the approach to Spahn Ranch; the Family appropriated Wilson's wardrobe, and just about everything else in sight; and several times Wilson found it necessary to take the whole Family to his Beverly Hills doctor for penicillin shots. "It was probably the largest gonorrhea bill in history," Dennis admitted. Wilson even gave Manson nine or ten of the Beach Boys' gold records and paid to have Sadie's [Susan's] teeth fixed." (*Helter Skelter*, pg. 339)

[40] "...during this time [fall 1968] we struck up a relation with Dennis Wilson of the famous Beach Boys. I was never sure how Charlie got to know him. It undoubtedly had something to do

The Hustle at Spahn Ranch

Family didn't pay rent anywhere it lived. The Family ate the day-old food discarded from supermarkets. The Family borrowed, and later began to steal, cars when it needed them. Except for drugs, and later guns, there were no expenses *at all* for the Family.

I believe it was this reliance on drugs and the money drugs brought in that began the cycle that led several months later to the murders of at least nine people.

The main problem about dealing drugs is also the most obvious – they are illegal. Being illegal, if you decide to pursue this vocation there is no better-business-bureau to turn to if you feel you have been cheated. And you will run into many people who are less than honorable. Charles Manson and the men in the Family began buying and then carrying guns.[41] The accounts given of life at Spahn Ranch tend to bare out the statement that guns appeared, not with the invent of Helter Skelter, but with the increased dealings with drug pushers and dealers. The fact is Charles Manson spoke of a black-white race war as far back as San Francisco and there weren't any guns at all at that time – they weren't needed.

---

with Charlie's own musical aspirations, plus our constant need for money." (*Child of Satan, Child of God*, pg. 113)

[41] "DeCarlo claimed he didn't know whose gun it was, but he said, "Charlie always used to carry it in a holster on the front of him. It was more or less always with him." " (*Helter Skelter*, pg. 140)

What you have building up is a recipe for disaster. An ever increasing appetite for an illegal substance that pushes Charles Manson further and further into illegal means of obtaining it. Robberies and swindles were performed, sometimes including very dangerous drug burns. And all to obtain more and more money for drugs. By the summer of 1969, Family members were being encouraged to steal from their friends and even burglarize their parents' homes to help make up for this drug deficit.

And the best part about all this, as far as Charles Manson was concerned, was that they were giving him the money and he didn't have to get near the crimes.[42] He thought he was faultless because he hadn't actually gone out and stole the money himself. This was a pattern he would try to use again later.

Charles Manson had long ago adopted the communist idea of shared property among the members of the Family. But here, once again, you can see the true motive. He told new indoctrinates they had to give up all worldly wealth and possessions to be truly free ...but they had to give these worldly possessions and wealth up to Charles Manson. And all so he could dress in expensive leathers and

---

[42] "...The best part was, with all the willing and skilled help I came up with, I didn't have to be at the scene of the crime. Nor did I have to set up scores or give orders. An occasional suggestion usually resulted in the goods being delivered." (*Manson, in His Own Words*, pg. 168)

maintain his psychotic drug state while the rest of us ate food out of dumpsters.

But how we faired didn't matter to Charles Manson. In his accounts of those days Manson is fond of stating everything he did was done "for those kids." The truth is he didn't do anything for the young people around him except live off them, brutalize them, molest them, and introduce them to criminal life. The extent to which he cared for the young people around him can be seen in the fact that he led seven of us to California's death row just to satisfy his own petty wants.

But by far, the most important change that happened during this period as far as I was concerned was the birth of my son on October 3rd, 1968. Though born two months premature and only weighing a pound and a half, he was absolutely wonderful. He was the only good thing that happened to me during that entire part of my life.

But the good could not outweigh the bad. The hustle was taking its toll. During the summer of 1969, you could see the house of cards beginning to shake. Everything at Spahn Ranch was by-the-skin-of-your-teeth. Just barely getting enough food. Finding replacement clothes. Getting the money Charles Manson demanded. Just barely getting the drugs everyone had been waiting for.

And to cover up this shadow of impending doom there developed an almost hysterical flippancy. A rebellious devil-may-care attitude. Almost a fatalism about it all.

If just one little thing went wrong...

The House Fell

When a house of cards teeters, one can only hold one's breath. And when the house finally collapses, it goes down fast.

From bad to worse. Already in a bind for money, and feeling the bite of the local police whose attention he wasn't able to avoid due to the ever increasing numbers of underage runaways that flocked to Spahn Ranch, Manson was under an increasing amount of pressure. In addition, the local bikers who were once friends were beginning to resent Manson for pulling their members away and they had actually threatened him several times.[43]

It was in the middle of this already tense situation that Manson started pressuring everyone

---

[43] [Al Springing told detectives] "...the Straight Satans held their club meetings on Friday, and they had discussed getting Danny [DeCarlo] away from Charlie. "A lot of the guys in the club were going to go up there and beat his ass, teach him a lesson not to brainwash our members..." Eight or nine of them did go to Spahn that night..." (*Helter Skelter*, pg. 125)

more and more for money. There are some indications Manson was already thinking of moving away in order to avoid the growing problems with police and bikers, and had sent people to scout out in the desert. But in order to move he needed more money, and everyone was pushed more and more to this end.

This is when the "Crowe incident" happened.

Bernard Crowe was a black drug dealer in the San Fernando Valley. What apparently happened, though neither I nor any of the others were privy to this at the time, was that in response to Manson's pressure Charles Watson had orchestrated a drug deal with Bernard Crowe. Apparently Watson convinced Crowe to give him the drugs, leaving his fiancé behind as security. Watson apparently told Crowe he would sell the drugs to a waiting buyer and then return immediately with the money.

But this isn't what happened.

I should mention that Charles Watson had taken a drug concocted by boiling hallucinogenic seeds earlier in the week and he wasn't himself during this whole episode. He'd disappear for long periods of time, or sit comatose for hours and have to be hand fed. I don't know what he'd taken but I remember it really messed him up. This may have had a very strong effect on what ended up happening.

Another thing worth noting is that the girl wasn't really his fiancé. He'd only just met her and apparently he decided to abandon her and run off with the drugs. Unfortunately the girl had heard Watson call Spahn Ranch earlier and she remembered the phone number. When Watson didn't come back Bernard Crowe began pressuring the girl and she gave him the number she'd seen Watson call. Crowe called and asked for "Charles." But Charles Watson was known as "Tex" at Spahn Ranch. There was only one "Charles," and that was Charles Manson. When Manson answered the phone Crowe told him he was a Black Panther (which wasn't true) and he knew where Manson was and if Manson didn't come down and give him his money he and all his Black Panther buddies were going to make a raid at Spahn Ranch and kill everyone there.

It's worth looking at the incident that followed – the Crowe Incident – a little closer, because it is the true beginning of the terrible panicked spiral that led to the deaths of nine innocent people.

Though Charles Manson had never even heard of Bernard Crowe it was immediately obvious that 1) Bernard Crowe knew who he was (this was a mistake in identification, but Charles Manson never figured this out), 2) Bernard Crowe knew where Charles Manson lived, and 3) Bernard Crowe was mad.

To Charles Manson this was no small problem. There was no way he could run from the police, the bikers, *and* the Panthers... he was broke. So he had to deal with Bernard Crowe one way or another. If he couldn't con Bernard Crowe, Charles Manson believed the only way to prevent the Panthers from getting his name and where-abouts was to eliminate the source – Bernard Crowe. If something happened to Crowe no one would be around to tell the Panthers *anything*. But either way, it had to be done quick.

And so Charles Manson told Bernard Crowe he would meet with him and straighten the whole thing up.

Manson got a gun and took one of the early members of the Family, a young man named T.J. Walleman, and he went down into the San Fernando Valley. The account given by T. J. later was that Charles Manson placed the gun in the back of his belt, so that it wouldn't be visible as he walked toward Crowe. The plan was that if Manson wasn't able to talk his way out of the situation, when they got close enough Manson would signal T. J., who was supposed to pull out the gun and shoot Bernard Crowe.[44]

This plan for killing Bernard Crowe gives a perfect insight into Charles Manson. *He* set up the meeting. *He* arraigned how it was to be carried out. And the arraignment was that if the dealer threatened

---

[44] "... I [prosecutor Bugliosi] did question T.J. as to the events immediately prior to [the shooting of Bernard Crowe]. He recalled how, after receiving a telephone call, Manson borrowed Swartz' '59 Ford, got a revolver, then, with T.J. accompanying him, drove to an apartment house on Franklin Avenue in Hollywood. After stopping the car, Manson handed T.J. the revolver and told him to put it in his belt." (*Helter Skelter*, pg. 473)

him, he'd get an innocent person to take the fall for killing Crowe. T.J. was a member of the very Family that Manson professed a willingness to die for, one of our "brotherhood" as he used to put it – a friend. And yet Charles Manson tried to get T. J. Walleman to kill Bernard Crowe.

This is the same basic tactic he would use later.

But this wasn't the way it happened.

According to the Prosecutor, when Manson got to Bernard Crowe's apartment there were several of his friends there. Manson tried to smooth-talk him, but when that didn't work and an altercation became inevitable Manson signaled T.J. to pull the gun. But T.J.'s better sense prevailed and he refused to pull the gun out of the back of Manson's belt. This left Manson standing all alone in the middle of Bernard Crowe's living room, in a predominantly black neighborhood, facing what he thought were several Black Panthers and one angry dope-dealer who'd just been ripped off.

Manson was forced to pull the gun himself. He shot Bernard Crowe right in the chest. Crowe fell to the ground and lay still. Manson and T. J. ran.

Later Bernard Crowe told police he'd played dead until Manson left and then got to a hospital. His friends had made sure Manson thought Crowe had been killed, probably to prevent Manson from coming back looking to complete the job. By the grace of God Bernard Crowe did not die, though according to the

The Myth of Helter Skelter

Prosecutor's account he was on the critical list for over two weeks. When questioned by police at the time of the shooting, Crowe insisted he didn't know who had shot him. One can only imagine he was more interested in taking care of Charles Manson himself when he got well.

It may be educating to look at the account that Manson himself gives of the events surrounding his attempted murder of Bernard Crowe. Charles Manson claims he went to Bernard Crowe's house not to kill him but to protect this mystery girl who, Charles Manson claims, Bernard Crowe was holding hostage until he got his money. According to Manson it was T.J. who decided to bring the gun with them. Once at the house, Bernard Crowe attacked Charles Manson and, in defense of his own life and the honor and virtue of this mystery girl (who Manson had never seen before) Charles Manson shot Bernard Crowe down while Crowe had him by the neck.

This version of the story sounds nothing like the versions told by anyone else and is so ridiculous it really has to be read to be believed. At one point, Charles Manson claims to have got down on his knees in front of Bernard Crowe and begged for the life of the girl, actually saying at one point, 'If you have to kill someone, then take me and let her go.'[45]

---

[45] "I dropped to my knees in front of his chair. "Look, man, I'm on my knees to you, please don't hurt the girl. I promise to

The House Fell

That Charles Manson, the accomplished Manipulator, ended up having to pull the gun and shoot Crowe himself is a testament to how foolish a position he'd put himself in. He had obviously thought he could get T. J. to take care of his dirty work for him.

That it hadn't worked and he'd had to dirty his hands infuriated Charles Manson. He was so angry and abusive to T.J. when they got back to Spahn Ranch that T.J., a long time member of the Family and a friend, left in the middle of the night out of fear for his life.[46]

The irony was that Charles Manson had thought he could keep his identity hidden from the Panthers by silencing Crowe quickly. But Bernard Crowe had been with friends when Charles Manson arrived. As

---

get your money. Just let the girl to." He laughed at me and said maybe he'd just rather kill the girl and watch her die instead of waiting for the money. Still kneeling, I took the gun from behind my back and held it butt first out to Crowe and told him, "Here, man, if you have to take a life, take mine." He looked at the gun for an instant before reaching for it. When he reached, I twirled it around so the handle rested in the palm of my hands and sprang to my feet." (*Manson in his Own Words*, softbound version, pg. 180 (Hardbound version, pgs. 170-176))

[46] "DeCarlo described T.J. as "a really nice guy; his front was trying to be one of Charlie's boys, but he didn't have it inside." T.J. had gone along with Mason on everything up to this but he told him, "I don't want to have nothing to do with snuffing people." A day or two later he "fled in the wind." " (*Helter Skelter*, pg. 141)

Charles Manson ran from the apartment a few moments later he believed that now, not only did the Panthers believe it was he who had ripped off Crowe, they would soon find it was he who had killed one of their brothers.

When Charles Manson returned to Spahn Ranch that night he still had to worry about where he was going to raise money for more drugs, and where he was going to make his connections, and whether the police were getting ready to move in on him over the auto thefts and under-age kids at the ranch. On top of all that he now had to worry about a murder charge and the prospect of being arrested.

Probably more disturbing to him that night was the prospect of retaliation by the Panthers for Crowe's death. That would not be good.[47]

---

[47] "Paranoia immediately set in. The police I had answers for, but the Black Panthers weren't about to let some score go unsettled. It meant war. Guns and learning how to use them instantly became a part of getting things together for the desert." (*Manson in His Own Words*, softbound pg. 182)

Chapter 7

Running and Money

It must have been obvious to Charles Manson that if he wanted to live he had to get away from Spahn Ranch. If Bernard Crowe had found him there then anyone could find him there, especially Crowe's friends.

But moving takes money. And the whole reason the Family had ended up in the old, dilapidated, fly-ridden movie ranch was because money was scarce (except, of course, for drugs). Charles Manson needed still *more money.* And he needed it immediately. But that's exactly how he had got into this mess in the first place.

Barker Ranch, out in Death Valley, had been located earlier in the year, maybe as early as late 1968. It had originally been considered as a home for the Family when it looked as though things at Spahn Ranch weren't going well. Charles Manson loved the desert. But the problem of just reaching the isolated ranch, let alone moving in enough food and supplies to feed the expanding Family, kept this move from being actualized. Now it looked as though this might be the answer to Charles Manson's problems. No one would be able to find him there.

But Charles Manson was not going by himself. He needed gunmen, and women to do chores for him. But in order to move the entire Family he desperately needed money – and now!

Chapter 8

The Lie that Wouldn't Die

Believing he had murdered Bernard Crowe, Charles Manson became frantic. He had, through his undying self-centeredness and an incredible underestimation of T.J.'s integrity, put himself in a position where he had dirtied his own hands. Immediately he had two huge additional problems. The first was that many of the people in and around Spahn Ranch knew he had gone to see Crowe. That meant there were possibly a dozen people who could corroborate any accusation against him. It was an incredible blunder for a boastful career criminal. Even among his loyal Family he must have felt as though a rope was coiling around his neck. And so he came up with a plan to protect himself from the very people he claimed he was willing to give his life for. We'll get to that later.

The second problem was much more subtle. Charles Manson needed people around him. He needed the women for sex, to make him feel important, to do chores for him, and to draw men into the Family.[48, 49] He needed men to deal his drugs, make his connections, rob and steal to raise money... and now for protection. But he could hardly admit he had just killed a Black Panther and the entire brotherhood of Black Panthers was about to come screaming into Spahn Ranch to wipe us all out. If he had said that everyone would have left. The Panthers weren't looking for any of the rest of us, just Charles Manson.[50]

So Charles Manson had to figure out how to turn Spahn Ranch into a fortress without letting anyone know the real reason.

And then it came to him. The answer was right before his eyes. It was right there in the apocalyptic sermons he had used to spell-bind the drug-enfeebled minds of the young men and women all the way back to the San Francisco days.

Vaguely taken from the Bible, enhanced slowly over months and months to include eastern mysticism, current social and political events, and even popular

---

[48] "It was only through the women, Gregg [Jakobson] said, that Charlie could attract the men. Men represented power, strength. But he needed the women to lure the men into the family." (*Helter Skelter*, pg. 302)

[49] "Linda [Kasabian] had already testified that Manson ordered the girls to make love to male visitors to induce them to join the Family..." (*Helter Skelter*, pg. 433)

[50] [Editor's Note: It should be mentioned once again that Bernard Crowe was not a Black Panther. But Charles Manson believed he was, and all his actions after the murder attempt on Crowe were based on the false belief that he was a Panther.]

The Lie that Wouldn't Die

music, Charles Manson's prophecies about Armageddon now had a use other than to bemuse young, idealistic minds. This vague and varying prophecy had even found a name for itself among the revolutionary sounds of the Beatles' White Album – Helter Skelter. The kids loved it. And after two years of modifying the tale Charles Manson could tell it with dramatic effect. It was perfect.

The beautiful part about it was that any amount of arming and preparations could be covered by the explanation that they were preparing for Helter Skelter. And Charles Manson's constant talk of a black/white race war provided excellent cover for telling his young idealistic followers to keep an eye out for blacks sneaking around Spahn Ranch. It all worked to perfection. His long, repetitive sermons every night began to be re-molded to reinforce the militant preparations.

This is the time period when more and more guns began to appear at the Ranch.[51, 52] This is also the time period when Manson had bowie knives

---

[51] [After shooting Bernard Crowe] "Guns and learning how to use them instantly became a part of getting things together for the desert." (*Manson in His Own Words*, softbound pg. 182)

[52] "Anticipating a move on us by the blacks, we collected all the guns we could get our hands on. Danny DeCarlo and some of the other guys around the ranch who were familiar with guns taught the kids to use them." (*Manson in His Own Words*, softbound pg. 185)

purchased and all the women were told they were supposed to carry them at all times.[53, 54, 55]

An incredibly crafty bonus of Charles Manson's Helter Skelter story was that it really drew the Family *together*. If facing an onslaught of Black Panthers the best defense would be to scatter. But if preparing for Armageddon there would be no use in running away. Safety would be in friends and sticking together.

To this day Mr. Bugliosi is still very adamant Helter Skelter was the motive for the crimes, but I am tempted to believe this is now more out of personal pride than out of reason. Vincent Bugliosi made his name on this case and to have to admit his motive might not have been correct, even after thirty-seven years, might make his victory look a little less impressive. None-the-less, there has been some evidence in the past years that even he is starting to

---

[53] "Everyone carried a knife [when creepy-crawling]." Quoting Susan. (*Helter Skelter*, pg. 235)

[54] "...Ruby, George's [Spahn's] ranch manager... told me [Bugliosi] that prior to the arrival of the Family at Spahn, she had never seen any Buck knives there, but that in the summer of 1969, "suddenly it seemed everyone had one."" (*Helter Skelter*, pg. 385)

[55] "In interviewing Danny [DeCarlo], I'd learned a great many things which were not on the LAPD tapes. For example, he recalled that in early August 1969, Gypsy had purchased ten or twelve Buck knives, which had been passed out to various Family members at Spahn." (*Helter Skelter*, pg. 479)

accept that Helter Skelter was only a con to get people to do what Charles Manson wanted them to do.[56]

The truth is Charles Manson said whatever he had to, to whomever he had to, to get them to do what he wanted them to do. To some he insisted the motive *was* Helter Skelter. That was what they responded to. For the more militant members of the Family the motive became revolution![57] To some he made it sound like a religious trial – a bloodletting that had to be borne. The most ridiculous story to date is the one he told Sandra Good and Lynette Fromme, and which (incredibly) they still defend – that all the murders were committed as some sort of militant

---

[56] Bugliosi: "I want to give you one footnote to the Helter Skelter thing. This is the philosophy that he instilled into the killers to work them up into an emotional lather so they're willing to kill for him. And they bought it. Wait a minute-- they bought it hook, line and sinker. Manson may not have believed in it-- Manson may not have believed it wholly himself. There were two other motivations that Manson had. One is passion and lust for murder. That was his religion, that was his credo. The second reason, he has an enormous amount of hostility towards society, against the establishment. And on these two nights of murder he was viciously striking out at the establishment and using his-- his minions to vent his spleen on society." (The Bertice Berry Show, Feb. 18, 1994, transcripts pg. 10 & 11)

[57] [Editor's Note: I believe this is true of Catherine Share, who's parents, I believe Bugliosi said, fought in the French resistance in WWII, and to whom the notion of Revolution would have seemed more romantic.]

The Myth of Helter Skelter

environmental protest.[58] That's what they needed to believe in order to get them to go along.[59]

Predictably enough, none of these odd stories is what Manson told the male followers who were close to him and who shared his confidence during the drug dealing.

I think the most decisive blow to the contention that Helter Skelter was the true motive for the killings was the fact Charles Manson told these men he had just killed a Panther and he needed money to split to the desert and he needed it *now*!

The reason I know this is because by the late summer of 1969, my son was over half a year old and I was becoming very attached to him. This was not

---

[58] Good [1994]: "What we were all about was to save our air. We have an organization called ATWA. It stands for Air, Trees, Water and Animals." (The Bertice Berry Show, Feb, 18, 1994, transcripts, pg. 1)

[59] "...it seemed we were never going to get the needed items for the desert. ... And seeing nothing moving us towards the desert, maybe I got a little surly with the kids. I started using anything I could that might convince them the desert was the only place for us." [There follows a long description of how he told the Family about underground rivers he'd seen and how they were going to turn the desert into a city.] "...Real madness is going to explode soon-- everything is going to be Helter Skelter. But that won't affect us, 'cause we'll be in a beautiful land that only we know how to survive in. To be ready, we need equipment and supplies by the tons. If we have to do a little stealing and hustling to get what we need, let's do it." (*Manson, in His Own Words*, pg. 171)

The Lie that Wouldn't Die

allowed by Charles Manson. Mothers were kept away from their own children under the pretense that parents put too much guilt and structure on children and that they should be allowed to grow up free.[60, 61] In truth it was an iron-clad way of ensuring the mother would do whatever Charles Manson told her to do.

In my case I became so persistent about seeing my son and trying to look after him that I was constantly being sent away from Spahn Ranch with the men when they went to take care of business. This not only meant I overheard things the other women didn't get a chance to, I was able to see how the explanations Charles Manson gave for what we were doing varied depending on who he was talking to. Specifically, I got to hear what he told the men – and he didn't waste *their* time with stories of Helter Skelter.

One of the advantages of my being kept away from the main group at Spahn Ranch was that I was not subjected to the endless hours of Manson's

---

[60] "The mothers were not allowed to care for their own children. They separated her and Tanya, Linda [Kasabian] explained, because they wanted "to kill the ego that I put in her" and "at first I agreed to it, I thought that it was a good idea that she should become her own person."" (*Helter Skelter*, pg. 349)

[61] "Her [Kasabian's] testimony was also at times very moving. Telling how Manson separated the mothers and their children, and relating her own feelings on being parted from Tanya, Linda said, "Sometimes, you know, when there wasn't anybody around, especially Charlie, I would give her my love and feed her."" (*Helter Skelter*, pg. 434)

sermons about preparing for the war to end all wars. This, coupled with knowing what the men knew about Crowe, allowed me to see the militant arming of the Family during the end of 1969 in a little more disturbing light. And with the benefit of hindsight, this allows me to understand what went on in a way many of those who were in the Family at the time still don't understand.

So, Charles Manson told the story of Helter Skelter to the women and young people, and he told the truth to his right-hand men. But the lie was born, and slowly it took on a life of its own, and within the next year and a half it would grow and then turn on its creator and wrap its tail around his neck and squeeze the breath out of him.

Chapter 9

Black Riders

Fate is sometimes extremely determined. And coincidence is sometimes suspiciously poignant. In Charles Manson's case it seemed the book had been written and sealed with that one bullet he'd put in Bernard Crowe. As if he wasn't already scared for his very life, within the week a group of black people showed up at Spahn Ranch to rent horses. That's what George Spahn did at his Ranch – he rented out horses to suburban families for an afternoon of fun. But to Charles Manson this appeared to be an advance scouting party for the Panthers. He was terrified.[62]

I thought he was crazy. They were obviously just tourists up to rent horses – women and smiling children. But Charles Manson didn't see it that way. Looking back it almost seems as though Fate was

---

[62] "On weekends George Spahn did a brisk business renting horses. Occasionally among the riders there would be blacks. Manson maintained they were Panthers, spying on the Family." (*Helter Skelter*, pg. 348-349)

giving Charles Manson one last good kick in the pants to push him over the edge and on the way to his inevitable downfall.

That night he called a meeting of his top men – he wanted money and he wanted it *now!*

Chapter 10

The Targeting of a Friend

I, of course, was not asked to the meeting – none of the women were. But, once again, I had been forced away from my son and out to where the men met. Because of this I was in the back room and within earshot when Charles Manson brought the subject up. He'd killed a Panther, he said. They were coming to get him. He wanted out and he wanted his protection – the entire Family – to come with him.

They mulled it over for a long time. No one had any money. If anyone they'd known had any money they would have stole it long ago. Manson was desperate and getting angry. He was particularly angry with Charles Watson. Manson had done all this *for them*, he insisted. He had gone to Crowe's place to protect *them* – to cover up for Watson's mistake – now they had to do something to protect him.

In truth Manson hadn't gone to Crowe's place for anybody but himself. It was in the interest of keeping his identity hidden from the Panthers that Charles Manson shot Bernard Crowe. That he would try to make the other men feel guilty, and imply that only Manson had the courage to do what had to be done, was not below him at all. But it was Charles Manson himself who had pressured Watson and the others into drug deals. This is what ultimately led him to the confrontation with Bernard Crowe. In the final analysis he can blame it on no one else.

It should also be mentioned that the reason why Charles Manson couldn't find anyone in all of Los Angeles who was willing to loan or give him enough money to flee, or to put him up for awhile until the heat died down, was because by the summer of 1969, Charles Manson had abused the friendship of everyone who'd ever tried to help him. He'd robbed some of these people, stolen from others, threatened others when they didn't give him what he wanted, and shamelessly lived off others until he'd abused his welcome everywhere. No one who had anything worth taking wanted him anywhere near them.

Finally the men at the meeting were reduced to grabbing at the faintest of straws. Bobby Beausoleil thought he remembered someone saying a friend of the Family's, a music teacher named Gary Hinman, had inherited a lot of money.[63][64] This didn't seem

---

[63] "Questioned about the murder [of Gary Hinman] Kitty [Lutesinger] said she had heard that Manson had sent Beausoleil and a girl named Susan Atkins to Hinman's home to get money from him." "On October 13, the day after they talked to Kitty, Sergeants Whiteley and Guenther questioned [Susan] She told them that she and Bobby Beausoleil were sent to Gary

The Targeting of a Friend

very likely to me. Gary lived in a little place down Topanga Canyon – nothing fancy. But that's all they could come up with.

Charles Manson said that Hinman was practically part of the Family – or at least he could be convinced to join the Family. If he joined the Family he could be expected to turn his inheritance over.

Since this was all they could come up with they decided to try it.

Later it became quite obvious Manson didn't really care if Hinman joined the Family, as long as Manson got his money.

Hinman's house to get some money he had supposedly inherited." (both quotes, *Helter Skelter*, pg. 102)
[64] "But Charlie told us that Gary had inherited $21,000." (*Child of Satan, Child of God*, pg. 120)

The Myth of Helter Skelter

Chapter 11

The Killing of a Friend

So it was decided that Bobby Beausoleil would ask Gary to join the Family.

Bobby was probably picked as the one to approach Gary for a couple reasons. Gary Hinman taught guitar and he'd shown both Beausoleil and Manson some techniques, so Bobby already knew him pretty well. What's more, there was talk that Gary might have been gay and was attracted to Bobby. I don't know if this was true, it may all have been in Manson's imagination. None the less this might also have influenced the decision to choose Bobby as the one to try to pursued Gary to join the Family.

But there may be another reason Bobby was chosen. Bobby and Manson were both the tentative leaders of the Family. At the time Manson met Bobby, Bobby already had a small "family" of his own including Leslie Van Houten, Catherine Share and several other girls. Since Bobby Beausoleil was ultimately arrested prior to the Tate-LaBianca crimes people often forget he was also a leader of the Family, and there was something of a power struggle between him and Manson. This competitive relationship would have allowed Manson to insinuate to Bobby that he, Manson, had done his part by intercepting Crowe, and now Bobby had to show he was an active leader as well.

It was also a way of assuring Bobby dirtied his hands, making it less likely he'd be willing to testify against Manson about Crowe.

Manson chose to send Mary Brunner and me along as well. This is probably partly because Gary Hinman knew both Mary and me, and he would be comfortable with us. But I'm convinced it was also because Mary and I both had infant sons back at Spahn Ranch – sons who could be used to prevent us from going to the police if anything happened.[65] And I think Manson knew something was going to happen.

Forgetting I was in the back room when he had been talking to the men – or perhaps not aware I had heard him – Manson told Mary and me we were going with Bobby to pick up some money Gary owed Manson. At the time I found it hard to believe Gary had any money at all, but off we went.

---

[65] "An even bigger question remained: "How could you leave your daughter in that den of killers?" ... Linda replied that she felt Tanya would be safe there, *just so long as she did not go to the police.*" [emphasis in original] (*Helter Skelter*, pg. 391)

The Killing of a Friend

I had grave misgivings about the trip. A day or two earlier Manson had approached me and challenged me to go down and kill Gary. If I hadn't overheard the conversation of the night before I would have assumed it was one of his mind games – "would you die for me? I would die for you. Would you kill for me?"

He'd started the conversation by suggesting that I wasn't a leader or a doer, that I should just stay in the background. He knew this would get to me. An expert at manipulation, he knew I strove for attention and validation. He knew that suggesting I learn to "stay in the background" would grate on me and make me want to prove him wrong. I could tell he was trying to goad me. That he suggested killing Gary Hinman, even with a joking smile, struck me with fear. Charles Manson often used these kinds of little games to test people.[66] If he was just testing me I would have to play up to him. But what if he wasn't just testing me?

I had told Manson I wouldn't kill Gary and he had laughed and walked away as though it was all just a mind game. But the episode left me very wary about the trip to Gary's.

---

[66] "...He [Watkins] recalled that once at Spahn Ranch, Charlie told Sadie [Atkins]: "I'd like half a coconut, even if you have to go to Rio de Janeiro to get it." Sadie got right up and was on her way out the door when Charlie said, "Never mind." It was a test." (*Helter Skelter*, pg. 319)

In the end my worst fears were realized.

Gary Hinman, a music teacher, a practicer of transcendental meditation, a pacifist with a truly gentle spirit who had gone out of his way to befriend and help Charles Manson and the Family, was killed for refusing to give up money which, it turned out, he never had.

The senselessness, callous nature of this killing will never cease to grieve and dumbfound me. What made this so cruel was that Gary Hinman had befriended Charles Manson about a year ago while helping to provide food and clothing for Manson's new-born son by Mary Brunner. Gary Hinman had even allowed Mary Brunner to use his address with the social services people instead of the dilapidated Ranch so they wouldn't take Manson's son away from her. The extent to which drugs can befuddle the mind and destroy one's priorities is incredible.

In hindsight, the death of Gary is perhaps the hardest thing to understand or make sense of.

After Gary declined to join the Family, and after he insisted he'd inherited no money, Bobby pulled a gun out (to the surprise of Mary and me) and demanded the money. When Gary continued to deny he had any, even after Bobby beat him up, Manson arrived with Bruce Davis and became so enraged he tried to cut Gary's head off with his machete. Manson missed but severed Gary's earlobe and opened up a cut along the side of his face.

Manson left, ordering Mary and me to stay behind and nurse Gary back to health. After a couple days it became obvious Gary certainly didn't have any money. Bobby was on the phone several times in heated discussions with Manson, but I never knew what they were talking about.

On the third day, Bobby ordered Mary and me into the back of the kitchen and he went out into the livingroom where Gary was and killed him.[67] Bobby then told us to wipe the house down to remove any fingerprints. Bobby took Gary's car and drove us back to Spahn Ranch.

What continues to puzzle me even after all these years is what Charles Manson said to Bobby Beausoleil on the phone that led Bobby to kill Gary. I will never know, but I can guess.

I imagine Manson had suggested Bobby be the one to go get the money from Gary because Charles Manson knew if push came to shove he could remind Beausoleil that he, Manson, had already killed someone in the name of the Family. That Bobby had been beat over the head all week long about how only Charles Manson had the guts to take care of Bernard Crowe can easily be imagined. After challenging and

---

[67] "Chief witness for the prosecution [at Beausoleil's second trial] was Mary Brunner ... who testified that she had witnessed Beausoleil stab Hinman to death." (*Helter Skelter*, pg. 395)

shaming Beausoleil for the better part of a week, Manson sent him off to Gary's.

It's impossible to tell, but there are several reasons to think that Manson had intended for Gary to be killed from the beginning.

For one thing, Manson's attack on Gary whether lethal or not assured that Gary would have gone to the police as soon as he was left alone. Even if Gary hadn't wanted to, he could not have turned up at an emergency ward with that injury without the police being called. Manson must have known that.

The fact that Manson sent Mary Brunner and me with Bobby is also interesting. On one side was the fact the Gary Hinman knew and liked all three of us. That Charles Manson picked friendly faces to try to talk Gary out of his money can not be a mistake. But on the other side, it bares pointing out that Mary Brunner and I were the only women at Spahn Ranch with babies. (Linda Kasabian hadn't arrived with her daughter yet.) This can not have been a mistake either. That these children were kept away from us and guarded was well known, as was Manson's penchant for using them to persuade us to do "what's best for you and the children." That Mary and I wouldn't flee the Family or talk no matter what happened at Gary's was assured as long as Manson had our children.

And finally, if Bobby killed Gary then Manson would have something on Bobby that would assure that Bobby wouldn't tell anyone that Manson had killed Bernard Crowe – Bobby's hands would be dirty too.

The crime was poorly thought out, but the manipulation was flawless.

There is one other thing worth noting at this point. Remember when I said Charles Manson had made a terrific mistake when shooting Bernard Crowe in part because so many people at Spahn Ranch knew he had gone to Crowe's that day, and there were now almost a dozen people who could corroborate any accusations against him? And remember I said he formulated a plan to protect himself? Well, I think this was the plan – if Charles Manson had his hands dirty then he was going to make sure *everyone* got their hands dirty.
This is a pattern that continued over the next couple months. When Manson heard that I wasn't able to hold the gun on Gary Hinman, Charles Manson made sure that I was included in the Cielo Dr. murders. When he heard that Linda Kasabian had run from the Cielo Dr. murders, Charles Manson made sure she was included on the night of the LaBianca murders. He shamed Bobby Beausoleil into committing the Hinman murder by pointing out that he, Charles Manson, had already shot Bernard Crowe (ostensibly for the Family). Then he shamed or psyched Charles Watson into the Cielo-LaBianca

killings by pointing to the "sacrifice" that he and Bobby Beausoleil had made for the Family with the Hinman murder (ostensibly to cover up Watson's mistake with Crowe). He then psyched out Steve Grogan into the Shea murder by pointing to Bobby Beausoleil and Watson. One by one everyone was dirtied.

Until no one was left to finger Manson.

Chapter 12

The Tightening Trap

From Charles Manson's point of view the genius of the plan to kill Hinman was that after he was killed the house would be arranged to look like black radicals had done the murder. The Black Panthers would be suspected and this would put heat on them. With the police coming down on them the Black Panthers wouldn't have time to worry about Charles Manson. Once again – the consummate manipulator. And once again Charles Manson's interests would be served.

But the Hinman murder was slip-shod. Manson wanted to distance himself from the crime, but this meant he had to tell others what to do – others who in the case of Mary and me didn't want to be there and who hadn't been told Manson's true motives and so couldn't properly carry out his ideas. Manson had told so many lies to different members of the Family about why the killings were taking place that no one had the same idea about what he wanted done. This problem would blow up in Charles Manson's face within a month.

But at the Hinman crime Bobby Beausoleil knew exactly what Manson had planned. He knew all about the drug burn and the shooting of Bernard Crowe. He also understood that the killing of Gary Hinman was supposed to look like a Panther hit to throw pressure on them so they wouldn't have time to come to the Ranch.

When Gary was killed Bobby made Mary and me clean the house of anything that showed we had been there. A vaguely revolutionary statement was left on the wall in Gary's own blood – "Political Piggy." And for the final touch Bobby Beausoleil made a bloody palm print on the wall in the form of a panther paw.

Since Charles Manson was desperate to get out of Spahn Ranch and head for the desert he needed vehicles. So Bobby Beausoleil was directed to make Gary Hinman sign over the registration slips for his two cars. That Bobby actually did this was very foolish – because it made him the prime suspect – but perhaps it shows even at that point Bobby Beausoleil didn't actually think Manson was going to insist he kill Gary. But this doesn't make much sense either, because Manson had already sliced Gary's face open from temple to chin with a machete, removing half of Gary's ear in the process – it was pretty obvious no matter how much Gary Hinman liked Bobby he was going to go to the police as soon as he got a chance.

To show his "devotion" to the Family, Charlie packed up his things and left unceremoniously the day after Gary was killed. He said he was just going out for a couple days but it was obvious he feared that the police would soon trace the murder to Spahn Ranch and so he was running for the hills.

Two days later the police still hadn't discovered Gary's body. But by now Bobby Beausoleil had begun thinking – he'd been careful to wipe his fingerprints from everywhere in the house where he might have put his hands, but couldn't he be identified by his bloody palm print as well? Of course he could. He raced back over to Gary's house and desperately tried to wipe the print from the wall, but apparently it wouldn't come off.

Back at Spahn Ranch Bobby Beausoleil must have been furious. He'd been pushed into this by Manson and now he felt caught. The possibility he'd been conned by Manson must have been in the back of his mind – no report of Bernard Crowe actually being found dead had been heard. No police had even come to ask questions about Crowe. And to top it all off Charlie had packed up and split. Beausoleil loaded up one of Gary's cars and took off immediately without telling anyone (including his pregnant girlfriend) where he was going.

Within a week he was arrested I believe in San Jose when police found him sleeping in Gary's car on the side of the road and ran the license number. That Bobby had the registration slip signed over to him might have saved him, but in his haste to leave the Ranch he'd driven off with not only his bloody clothes in the trunk but with the knife he'd used to kill Gary as well.

Back at Spahn Ranch Charles Manson looked white as a ghost when he heard. If the charges stuck Beausoleil might try to bargain with the DA. And what did Bobby Beausoleil have to bargain with? How about Bernard Crowe. Charles Manson must have felt as though his foot was caught in the door.

Chapter 13

Selling Your Soul to Save Your Skin

When Bobby Beausoleil was transferred to Los Angeles County Jail, Charles Manson sent people to go talk to him. It can only be imagined that Bobby Beausoleil gave them an earful to report back to Manson. The gist of Bobby's comments was probably, "take care of this or I'm not going down alone."

That Manson was truly scared can be appreciated only by looking at his situation. He still had the police and the motorcycle gang breathing down his back. The Panthers were still as real and imminent a threat in his mind as ever. He still had his hands all over the Crowe shooting.[68] But now Charles Manson couldn't even run to the desert. As long as Beausoleil was in jail accused of the Hinman murder,

---

[68] [Manson on the drive back to Spahn Ranch after shooting Bernard Crowe] "I was sure the police would be coming to the ranch for me within hours..." (*Manson in His Own Words*, softbound pg. 182)

Charles Manson was stuck. If Manson made a run for it Bobby would assume Manson was throwing him to the lions and Bobby might start thinking of making a deal with the police.

To add insult to injury, the Hinman murder was not being associated with the Black Panthers *at all*. And it never was. The police hadn't the slightest idea what the bloody hand print was supposed to mean.

If Charles Manson had felt hunted before, now he was trapped *and* hunted. He couldn't go back to jail now, the joint was filled with Black Panthers. Charles Manson wouldn't last a week if they found out about Crowe.

Almost immediately after getting Bobby's messages Manson drew the Family together. He was more agitated than ever before. "The Family *has* to get Bobby out," he said. "He's our brother! We'll do anything to get our brother out of jail!" In hindsight it is obvious that it was Charles Manson who *had* to get Bobby out of jail. And not because he was our "brother" either.

But almost immediately Manson ran into trouble. Most of the Family had no idea what Bobby had actually done. Those who did still had completely different ideas about why Gary had been killed. Manson had told everyone something different. Now those lies were coming back to him. He certainly couldn't tell them the truth. He didn't want to implicate himself in the Crowe matter any more than possible. He fell back to preaching about coming atrocities and Armageddon. Perhaps he was talking more about his own impending doom than anything else – it must have seemed as obvious to him now as a monster about to swallow him whole.

But the stories no longer made any sense. Their references to the Bible and mythical stories were disjointed and didn't follow. It was only by his own desperate intensity that he made the reasoning unquestionable. I saw the fear and desperate anxiousness in him – the spark that could turn so quickly into a violent rage. He sounded insane. But I wasn't going to question him. I'd seen him cut Gary Hinman's face open from brow to chin. And Gary had been a *friend* of Manson's.

I knew I'd never been a friend.

I wasn't going to say anything. But I started keeping my eyes open and looking for a way out.

The Myth of Helter Skelter

Chapter 14

A Desperate Plan

The idea that the Cielo-LaBianca murders were in direct response to Charles Manson's fear of Bobby Beausoleil rolling over on him – the copycat motive – is convincingly supported by the fact that on the morning of Friday August 8, 1969, Charles Manson sent Mary Brunner and Sandra Good out to buy escape supplies, including rope, for a breakout attempt at the Los Angeles County Jail.

By mid-afternoon the word came back that Brunner and Good had been arrested for trying to buy the supplies with a stolen credit card.

This should give the reader an indication of just how hard up for money Charles Manson was. He had *counted* on that money from Gary Hinman. The District Attorney's investigation showed that it was during this time that Charles Manson even went back to beg the money from Dennis Wilson, the drummer for the Beach Boys – a long time supporter of Manson's who, when he told Manson he didn't have that kind of money laying around, was threatened with the death of his son.[69]

It had been over a week and a half since Gary Hinman's death and Charles Manson was at his wit's end. He was staying up for days at a time on drugs watching for Panthers. Guards were now posted all around Spahn Ranch, on the roofs of the buildings, on 24-hour watch.[70] The women began to fear for their lives as paranoid, speed-frazzled gunmen combed the ranch pointing hand guns and rifles with shaking hands at anyone who made a loud noise. And now Mary and Sandra were in jail.

---

[69] "Dennis [Wilson] told me that he didn't have any trouble with Charlie until August of 1969 – Dennis could not recall the exact date, but he did know it was after the Tate murders – when Manson visited him, demanding $1,500 so he could go to the desert. When Wilson refused, Charlie told him, "Don't be surprised if you never see your kid again." Dennis had a seven-year-old son, and obviously this was one reason for his reluctance to testify. ...Manson also threatened Wilson himself, but Dennis did not learn of this until an interview I conducted with both Wilson and Jakobson. According to Jakobson, not long after Dennis refused Manson's request, Charlie handed Gregg a .44 caliber bullet and told him, "Tell Dennis there are more where this came from." Knowing how the other threat had upset Dennis, Gregg hadn't mentioned it to him." (*Helter Skelter*, pg. 340)

[70] "At night everyone was required to wear dark clothing, so as to be less conspicuous, and eventually Manson posted armed guards, who roamed the ranch until dawn." (*Helter Skelter*, pg. 349)

A Desperate Plan

Bobby was not a fourteen-year-old girl Manson could threaten or seduce into silence. And if Bobby started to think he was set up or that Manson wasn't doing whatever he could to get him out, there was no telling what he might do. Manson, on the other hand, had promised himself he was not going back to prison. He knew very well that going to prison for killing a Black Panther would be a death sentence.

There was only one other way for Manson to get Bobby off the hook for the Hinman murder and thereby save his skin. That evening he decided to put plan B into effect.

The Myth of Helter Skelter

Chapter 15

Into the Maelstrom

Manson was very careful who he sent the night of August 8th, 1969. Once again he took care, first, to choose people who couldn't say no. Charles Watson was young and quiet. He, like Bobby had been worked on for over a week about how Manson and Bobby had gone the distance for the Family. He was chemically dependent. He was beat over the head again and again with the fact that all this had started because of the drug burn that he, Watson, was in charge of and which had led the Black Panthers to Spahn Ranch. It was easy to guess the extent to which Manson made Watson feel he *owed* Manson.[71, 72, 73]

---

[71] [After shooting Bernard Crowe] "...I had a score to settle with Tex. It was his burn, he got the money and it was a cross he belonged in, not me." (*Manson in His Own Words*, softbound pg. 182)

[72] [Manson to Watson after the Bernard Crowe shooting] "What you have done is to bring the Black Panthers down on us."... "What I did for you last night put our whole circle in a cross with the blacks. I saved your life by putting mine on the

The second thing Manson was careful to do was to pick people who didn't have their hands dirty yet. And that is why I was chosen. Linda Kasabian and Patricia Krenwinkel were pushed into the car for the same reason. Though Linda had only been in the Family for a month or two, she was picked for the same reason I had been sent to Gary Hinman's – her two-year-old daughter was being kept by Charles Manson in a separate area of the ranch "for her safety." [74] Patricia Krenwinkel was chosen because she had nowhere to run to. She couldn't have left the Family no matter what Manson did.

These choices were all deliberate. Calculated. Cold. His manipulation was expert once again, but his

---

line. Now it looks like all of us are in for it because of your shit. You owe us, brother!" (*Manson in His Own Words*, softbound pg. 182)

[73] "Tex, you remember the black and what I told you when I came home after killing him?" ... "That life I took for you was your life. Bobby is my brother. He is your brother. And to save our brother, I'm asking you for the life you own me." (*Manson in His Own Words*, softbound pg. 196)

[74] [Susan's Note: The assertion that Manson was knowingly using the children as a way of manipulating their mothers is further enforced by the fact that when we came back from the night of the Cielo Dr. crime Linda Kasabian and I discovered that while we'd been gone Manson had decided to move the children to a "safer" place further up Trabuco Canyon Road... where the police couldn't find them if they raided the Ranch and where we couldn't get to them if we decided to try to steal them away and make an escape. This relocation wasn't an accident.]

criminal planning was as faulty as with the killing of Gary Hinman.

Once again, one of Manson's main problems was that he was still trying to avoid admitting to anyone he had shot, and presumably killed, a Black Panther. And so the manipulations began again. The killings were done for revolution... no, they were done for the environment... no, they were done because we all just loved Bobby that much... no, they were done to start Helter Skelter... In reality they were instigated by Charles Manson to save his own skin. And it very quickly became obvious how expendable the "love of the Family" was to him. We were to do his dirty work and then, if worse came to worse, be thrown to the fire like a human sacrifice to the Justice Department to pay for the sins of Charles Manson.

So the bungling began. Charles Manson sent Watson to do a copycat killing just like the killing of Gary Hinman. But Watson had never been to Gary Hinman's house. He didn't know anything about the killing. All he knew was that it was horrible. Bobby hadn't stuck around long enough to do much describing other than to say that it was a terrible mess and that Hinman had been stabbed to death. Charlie himself knew little about the actual scene, and so he simply told Watson to "make it as gruesome as possible."[75, 76] Remembering that something had been

---

[75] [From Tex Watson's testimony at his trial] "Charlie called me over behind a car... and handed me a gun and a knife. He

The Myth of Helter Skelter

written on the wall in Gary Hinman's blood, Manson simply told the me and the other girls, "write something witchy."

But we still didn't know exactly what was going on. Pat, Linda and I knew nothing about threats by the Black Panthers. We didn't know that these murders were supposed to throw suspicion back on the Panthers. All we knew was a vague story about Helter Skelter, or revolution, or that these people were establishment people that should be hated.

We weren't even told what was going to happen, we were simply told to go with Charles Watson and do what he said.[77, 78]

---

said for me to take the gun and knife and go up to where Terry Melcher used to live. He said to kill everybody in the house as gruesome as I could. I believe he said something about movie stars living there." (*Helter Skelter*, pg. 627 & 628)

[76] "Tex [Watson] said that Manson's hold on him was complete, and he only murdered on Manson's orders... Tex said that when they entered the Sharon Tate house they didn't know who was going to be present. Manson had ordered them to kill everyone at the Terry Melcher home. ..." (*God's Prison Gang*, pg. 35)

[77] "...Manson told Linda, "Go with Tex and do whatever Tex tells you to do." According to Linda, in addition to Tex, Katie, and herself, Brenda McCann and Larry Jones were present when Manson gave this order." (*Helter Skelter*, pg. 350)

[78] "According to Linda, Tex did not tell them their destination, or what they were going to do; however, she presumed they were going on another creepy-crawly mission." (*Helter Skelter*, pg. 351)

Once we got to the Cielo Dr. house, because I had been at the Hinman house I was told to copy whatever had been written on the wall there. But all I could remember was "Pig," or that is all I could write without becoming physically sick. But it was not "Political Piggy," which was what had been written at Gary Hinman's house. A paw print was not left, but the reason here should be obvious – that's what Bobby Beausoleil believed got him caught. In fact, nothing of a revolutionary nature was left this time. The killings were so "witchy" that no one had any idea what the motive was. In truth, the reason there was no obvious motive was because the people Charles Manson sent didn't really know what they were supposed to be doing.

The outcome was that, just as with the Hinman killing, no one ever suspected the Black Panthers of the crime. What's even more pathetic and definitely worse for Charles Manson was that the killings were so "gruesome" (to use Charles Manson's word) that, other than the fact that a knife had been used, they didn't resemble the Hinman crime at all.

The next night the same thing. Once again Charles Manson hand picked the people he wanted to go.[79] Charles Watson and Patricia Krenwinkel would

---

[79] MANSON: "After dinner that evening [August 9th, 1969], he and six others ...stuffed ourselves into Swartz's old Ford and went searching for victims, random victims, so many of them that the deaths would shock not only the area but the whole world." (*Manson, in His Own Words*, pg. 208)

take Leslie Van Houten out to dirty her hands. And, because of our poor showing the night before, Linda Kasabian (who had run away) and I (who had lost my knife at the house and then froze) were forced to go again, this time taking Steve Grogan to dirty his hands.

Leslie was specifically picked because she was originally one of Bobby Beausoleil's girls. Charlie wanted to make sure that, just in case her loyalty turned back to Bobby and she decided to testify against Charles Manson at Bobby's trial, Manson would have something on her.

Steve Grogan was picked because he was one of the men who had already heard about the Crowe shooting. He had also been on the boardwalk of Spahn Ranch when we had returned from Cielo Dr. with blood on the car's door handles and steering wheel. Grogan already knew too much and Manson wanted to make sure that, just in case Grogan ever thought about talking, Grogan would know he had something to lose as well. Manson wanted him all the way in or all the way out.

But the killings the night before hadn't been what Manson had wanted. They hadn't been "done right," as Manson put it. The news reports didn't even mention a connection to the Hinman crime. Though Manson still wanted to distance himself from the killings as much as possible, so he could slip away if the police ever caught up to the Family, he felt he had to go along to show everyone what he had expected.[80] At the LaBianca residence he actually tied the couple up and robbed them, slipping out just before they were killed. That this action alone made him guilty of conspiracy as well as two counts of first degree murder shows his bungling – it also shows how unsophisticated he was about the law.

But Charles Manson still knew less about how the Hinman murder was carried out than Mary Brunner or myself. He insisted in directing us in copying a murder about which he himself knew almost no details. The only thing Charles Manson knew for sure about the murder of Gary Hinman was that he'd had his ear cut off. But Manson didn't remember to copy this!

Once again, the LaBianca killings were much more extreme than the killing of Gary Hinman. For one thing, Leslie Van Houten hadn't participated during the killings, so she was told to go back after the crime and do more. This led to the problem (a problem as far as Charles Manson's copycat plan was concerned) that this crime had ten times the number of wounds as the crime at Gary Hinman's.

Once more, writing was left in blood. But this time *no one* who'd been at the Hinman residence was there to help make any similarities. Patricia

---

[80] "When we left the ranch, I had been geared to handle some of the dirty work. The kids had done their thing last night [August 8th, 1969], and I was going to perform for them tonight." (*Manson, in His Own Words*, pg. 212)

Krenwinkel thought she remembered something about "pigs," but she wasn't sure what it was. "Death to pigs," "rise," and "healter skelter" were left instead. They sounded vaguely revolutionary. But Manson's reluctance to let anyone really know what was going on backfired on him again – the reference to the Beatles' song Helter Skelter not only completely eliminated the Black Panthers as suspects, it was Manson's own calling card. The bungling goes on.

To put further suspicion on the Black Panthers and convince the police the LaBianca killings were related to the Hinman case, Manson stole Ms. LaBianca's wallet and Linda Kasabian hid it in a gas station bathroom in a predominantly black neighborhood.[81] Unfortunately she hid it so well it wasn't found until long after we were all arrested.

Not only wasn't this crime associated with the Black Panthers or the murder of Gary Hinman... it appeared to be so different that it wasn't even associated with the Cielo Dr. crimes.[82]

---

[81] "Manson told Linda that when they reached a predominantly colored area he wanted her to toss the wallet out onto a sidewalk, so a black person would find it, use the credit cards, and be arrested." (*Helter Skelter*, pg. 365)

[82] [Susan's Note: Though it is not important now, on the night of the LaBianca crime Manson drove Linda Kasabian, Steve Grogan and I to the site of a second planned killing. Manson dropped us off and then left and we did not follow through.]

Into the Maelstrom

By the end of the weekend, seven more innocent people were dead. But more to Manson's interest, he'd managed to suck another eight members of his own Family into the depravity of his own soul just to make sure they couldn't turn him over about the shooting of Bernard Crowe.

Spahn Ranch was now in complete paranoia. Guns, knives, suspicion was everywhere. There was still no money. There were still Panthers out there. The bikers actually came up to the ranch looking to beat up Manson and he only scared them away with riflemen up on the roofs.[83] The men practiced shooting out behind the ranch every day. The women were instructed to wear their knives.[84, 85, 86] Everyone

---

[83] [Al Springing told detectives] "...the Straight Satans held their club meetings on Friday, and they had discussed getting Danny [DeCarlo] away from Charlie. "A lot of the guys in the club were going to go up there and beat his ass, teach him a lesson not to brainwash our members..." Eight or nine of them did go to Spahn that night, "but it didn't happen that way." Charlie had conned some of them. The girls had lured others into the bushes. And when they started breaking up things, Charlie told them that he had guns trained on them from the rooftops. Springer had one of his brothers check the gunrack that Charlie had shown him on his first visit. A couple of rifles were missing." (*Helter Skelter*, pg. 125)

[84] "In interviewing Danny [DeCarlo], I'd learned a great many things which were not on the LAPD tapes. For example, he recalled that in early August 1969, Gypsy had purchased ten or twelve Buck knives, which had been passed out to various Family members at Spahn." (*Helter Skelter*, pg. 479)

was supposed to wear dark clothing.[87] Strangers, even hippies, were no longer welcome.

Everything was coming apart so quickly. Charlie was walking around with his eyes wide open, double and triple checking his tracks to make sure he couldn't be caught.[88] Did everyone wipe their fingerprints off? Did everyone get rid of their bloody clothing? Were the knives and gun discarded far from Spahn Ranch? Were the knives wiped clean of prints before being discarded?

Things were bad. Real bad. It was as though we were drowning – always a sick feeling inside.[89]

---

[85] "...Ruby, George's [Spahn's] ranch manager. ...and told me that prior to the arrival of the Family at Spahn, she had never seen any Buck knives there, but that in the summer of 1969, "suddenly it seemed everyone had one."" (*Helter Skelter*, pg. 385)

[86] "He [Crockett] added that "all the women have been programmed to do exactly as he says, and they all have knives. ..."" (*Helter Skelter*, pg. 315)

[87] "At night everyone was required to wear dark clothing, so as to be less conspicuous, and eventually Manson posted armed guards, who roamed the ranch until dawn." (*Helter Skelter*, pg. 349)

[88] "This incident had occurred in late August or early September of 1969. Jakobson was startled by the change in Manson. "The electricity was almost pouring out of him. His hair was on end. His eyes were wild. The only thing I can compare it to... is that he was just like an animal in a cage."" (*Helter Skelter*, pg. 340)

[89] "[Investigator's questioning of Susan in 1969] "How did you feel about what you had just done?" [Answer] "I almost

And I think that's how Manson must have felt – as though he just barely had his head above water. If there was even the slightest ripple, he knew he'd go under.

---

passed out. I felt as though I had killed myself. I felt dead. I feel dead right now.'"" (*Helter Skelter*, pg. 243)

The Myth of Helter Skelter

Susan leaving the Grand Jury room with Richard Caballero after testifying against Charles Manson.

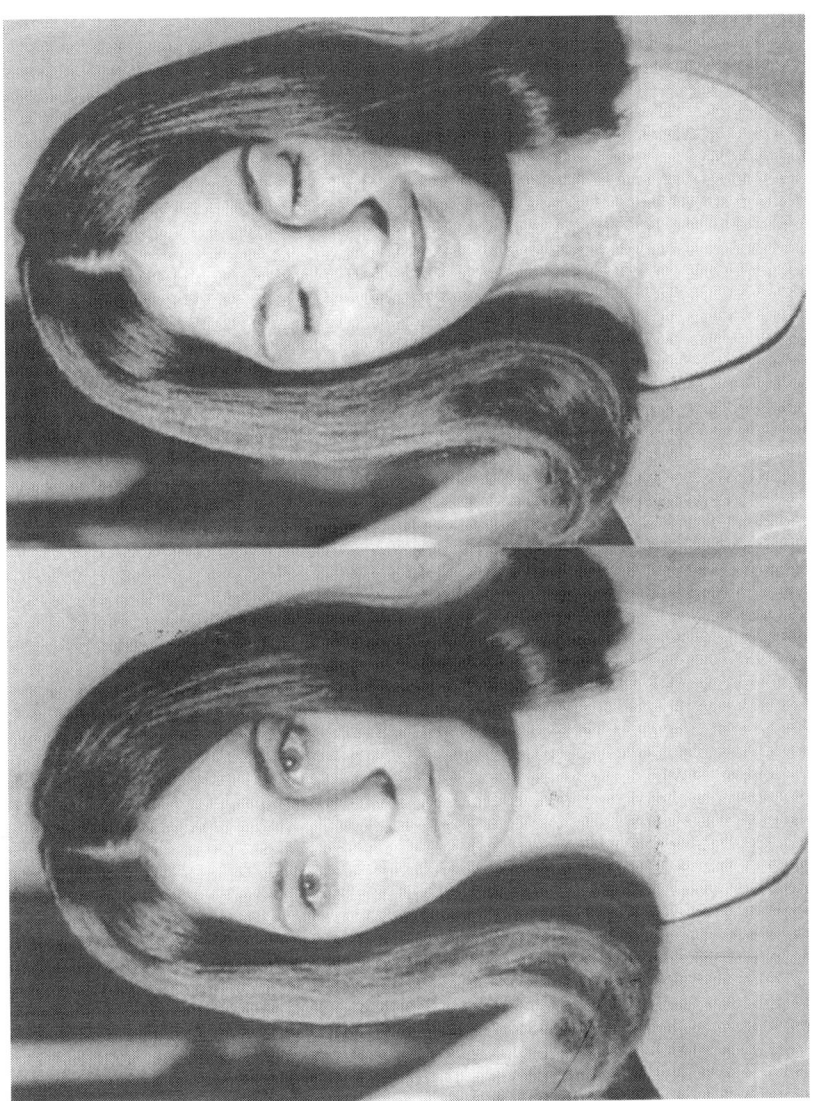

Newspaper photographs taken as Susan left the Grand Jury room. The hallway was filled with photographers - something that seemed ridiculous to Susan.

The Myth of Helter Skelter

Patrician Krenwinkel, Susan, and Leslie Van Houten being led to court during the trial. This was after Susan recanted her Grand Jury testimony and was trying to fit back in.

This is picture was shot on one of the outings when Susan was taken out to help the police try to find evidence in the case. By 2008 the LA DA's Office insisted this never happened. Susan has the LA jail bracelet visible on her left writ. (photo: Rory White)

The Myth of Helter Skelter

Susan in one of the stark prison buildings about 1993. After all those years of turmoil she found peace and strength in God and spent her life helping others. At her 2005 parole hearing one of the victims' family members said "I am 60 years old and I don't know of anybody that has done all of these things [Susan has]."

Chapter 16

The Sickening Sigh of Relief

Once again, the contention that Charles Manson's motive was to save his own skin by getting Beausoleil off the Hinman charge so Beausoleil wouldn't be tempted to implicate Manson is borne out by the fact that the very next day Manson sent Linda Kasabian to go visit Bobby Beausoleil in jail. The message Manson told her to give was a simple one – Don't say anything. Everything's been taken care of.[90]

And Spahn Ranch breathed a sigh of relief. But the churning sickening feeling stayed. For Charles Manson the killings represented no more than a calculated risk. To those in the Family who had been ordered to carry them out they were horrific, traumatic experiences that would not go away. And Spahn

---

[90] "Early the next morning (August 12) Manson sought her [Kasabian] out. She was to put on a "straight" dress, then take a message to Mary Brunner and Sandra Good at Sybil Brand, as well as Bobby Beausoleil at the County Jail. The message: "Say nothing; everything's all right." (*Helter Skelter*, pg. 389)

Ranch became a ghost town, with half-dead, shocked specters drifting between the buildings.

This is a fundamental difference between Charles Manson and all the other co-defendants related to these crimes. As far as I know Charles Manson is the only one who has never shown any remorse. All the other co-defendants have, at some time over the last thirty five years, gone through a complete emotional and psychological breakdown over what they witnessed and were a part of.[91, 92, 93] I don't know if the true horror of those nights has ever struck him.

---

[91] [Susan's Note: After the crimes, Watson had a complete breakdown and went catatonic for more than a week – having to be hand fed, bathed and even taken to the bathroom by others.]

[92] "Of the three, [Dr.] Hochman felt Sadie had a little more remorse than the other two – she often talked of wishing her life were over. ... And he testified, "She does not seem to manifest any evidence of discomfort or anxiety about her present circumstances, or her conviction and possible death sentence. On the contrary, she seemed to manifest a remarkable peacefulness and self-acceptance in her present state." (*Helter Skelter*, pg. 601)

[93] "Had that Los Angeles reporter been right? Someone had told me what he wrote, probably Leslie or Pat. Was he right? "Watching her behavior—bold and actressy in court, cute and mincing when making eyeplay with someone—I get the feeling that one day she might start screaming, and simply never stop." (*Child of Satan, Child of God*, pg. 179)

The Sickening Sigh of Relief

And so, convinced that he'd freed himself from the threat of Bobby throwing him to the wolfs, Charles Manson relaxed... a little. There was still the need to get away from the Ranch as soon as could be managed.

Vehicles were being stolen and converted for desert use as quickly as possible. Charles Manson had expectations of making it to the desert within weeks.

But it didn't happen.

On August 16th, the police swarmed into Spahn Ranch with a warrant for evidence connecting us all to auto theft. And everyone ended up in jail. Manson must have had a heart-attack when he saw those police flashlights. Even once he was assured the arrests were only for auto theft there must have been an eerie forewarning as he was locked up in County Jail. He must have felt like he couldn't breathe.

The Myth of Helter Skelter

Chapter 17

A New Desperation

The auto theft arrests were eventually thrown out because the search warrant was old. That Charles Manson would have breathed a sigh of relief can only be imagined. If he did, it was a short one. Once back at the Ranch he became possessed with the plan to get out to the desert. The time in jail must have really shook him up.

To get a true understanding of Charles Manson it is worth pointing out that when arrested he was still holding Linda Kasabian's two-year-old daughter as security against her going to the police. Linda had stolen one of the vehicles from the Ranch and was able to escape prior to the police raid but only by abandoning her daughter.[94] When everyone was put in jail the child became a ward of the courts, as did my

---

[94] "An even bigger question remained: "How could you leave your daughter in that den of killers?"... Linda replied that she felt Tanya would be safe there, *just so long as she did not go to the police.*" [emphasis in original] (*Helter Skelter*, pg. 391)

son. When Linda Kasabian found out about the arrests she figured it would be safe to sneak back to Los Angeles and get her daughter from the courts without anyone from the Family finding out. According to the prosecutors account she was horrified to hear from the case worker that a young woman had already showed up to claim the child but was refused when she couldn't provide any identification.[95]

This shows that Charles Manson knew exactly why he was holding on to those children. It was no coincidence that Linda Kasabian's child, as well as my own and that of Mary Brunner, were moved away from Spahn Ranch just at the time of the murders. It was not out of concern for the children that they were kept under guard night and day. It was a calculated,

---

[95] "[After she escaped Spahn Ranch] Linda did not talk to Charlie [on the phone], but she did talk to one of the other girls – she believed, but was not sure, it was Squeaky – who told her about the August 16 raid. The authorities had kept Tanya, she learned; she was now in a foster home. ...Linda subsequently called the Malibu police station and learned the name of the social worker who was handling Tanya's case." [footnote] "On calling the social worker, Linda learned that another girl, passing as Tanya's mother, had attempted to reclaim Tanya a short time before. Though I couldn't prove it, I suspected that Manson had sent one of his girls to get Tanya, as insurance that Linda wouldn't talk." (*Helter Skelter*, pg. 390)

and brutal, form of manipulation. They were Charles Manson's security policy.⁹⁶

Once out of jail, the first order of the day for Charles Manson was retribution. Donald "Shorty" Shea had been a ranch hand at Spahn Ranch ever since the Family moved there the year before. He'd always been on cordial terms with Manson, but when Shea begun to suspect that stolen cars were being stripped in the back of the ranch his attitude changed. This had been right around the time Bernard Crowe had been shot. Now Manson's frustration and anger were vented on Donald Shea.

Whether Donald Shea actually had anything to do with the police raid or not has never been proved. I suspect if he had anything to do with it Vincent Bugliosi would have found out and used it against Manson at the trial. But then, Shea's actual involvement didn't really matter, what's important was that Manson *thought* Shea was responsible for the raid.⁹⁷ And the raid had sent Manson back almost to

---

⁹⁶ [After the LaBianca crime, Kasabian told prosecutors] "They [Kasabian, Grogan and Susan] then hitched two rides [after Venice], the last taking them all the way to the entrance of Santa Susana Pass road, where Clem [Grogan] and Linda got out. Sadie [Susan], Linda learned the next day, remained in the car until it reached the waterfall area. [Where she believed the children had been moved.]" (*Helter Skelter*, pg. 368)

⁹⁷ "Charlie also suspected that Shorty had helped set up the August 16 raid on Spahn [DeCarlo thought] – Shorty was

square one as far as getting out of Spahn Ranch. In fact it set him back even more, because now the police hung all over the Ranch just waiting for someone to step out of line.

Manson struck back. Shea was reportedly decapitated and cut into pieces out behind the Ranch and then buried in several deep holes. His body wasn't discovered until almost seventeen years later when Steve Grogan agreed to cooperate with authorities.[98]

Once again, Manson arranged the killing for his own purposes. The main participant was Steve Grogan, who did not get his hands dirty on the night the LaBiancas were killed. That Grogan ended up dragged into murder was important to Manson because Grogan not only knew about Crowe, he now knew about the LaBianca killings and he watched Manson greet those coming back from the Cielo Dr. murders. The back-up cast – those who either lured

---

"offed" about ten days later. And there was the possibility, though this was strictly conjecture on DeCarlo's part, that Shorty had overheard something about some of the other murders." (*Helter Skelter*, pg. 144)

[98] [Editor's Note: It's important to mention that when Grogan cooperated with authorities and Donald Shea's body was uncovered, it was not mutilated or decapitated at all. The story that Charles Manson had circulated about the mutilation was simply another tool of manipulation to dissuade Family members from thinking of talking to the police or of trying to run away. See *Helter Skelter*, AFTERWORD, pg. 509.]

Shea out behind the Ranch or helped clean up and bury him afterwards – included just about everyone not involved up to this point; Catherine Share, Nancy Pitman, Sandra Good and Lynette Fromme.

Charles Manson's safety net - his ability to blackmail anyone who knows about his shooting Bernard Crowe - was almost completely in place.

It goes without saying this period was nothing like the love-filled days in San Francisco or the first year in Los Angeles. That the atmosphere was still anything like communal is ridiculous. Those who could leave, did. Linda Kasabian had already abandoned her daughter and fled.[99] The friend I had traveled to Los Angeles with, Ella-Jo – one of the original six girls in the Family – had disappeared with her boyfriend without a word one morning after Gary Hinman was killed. She didn't say good bye to anyone.[100]

T.J. split immediately after the Crowe incident. Patricia Krenwinkel disappeared shortly after the Shea

---

[99] "Linda saw her chance [to escape Spahn Ranch] ...she went to get Tanya, but discovered that the children had been moved to the waterfall area. There was no way she could go there to get Tanya, she said, without having to explain her actions. So she left the ranch without her." (*Helter Skelter*, pg. 389)

[100] "Ella Jo Bailey was eliminated [as a possible conspirator to the Cielo-LaBianca crimes]; she'd left Spahn ranch before the murders." (*Helter Skelter*, pg. 148)

murder.[101] Charles Watson stood up out of his nearly comatose state one day and simply vanished. Bruce Davis went into hiding. Paul Watkins ran off from the Family's desert ranch.

By the time the Family was arrested in the desert, a month or two in the future, only a dozen or so members still remain out of a Family that at one time held almost forty.

Finally, ready or not, the Family was moved to the desert. Manson could have gone much sooner on his own, but he was afraid to move without his bodyguard of followers. Supplies were sparse and conditions rough. More people tried to leave. Some were hunted down in the desert and brought back. Others were caught up to where ever they surface and warned to tell no one what they'd seen or heard.

In Charles Manson's mind the Panthers were now far behind. But the police are not. Caches of arms and gasoline are stored out in the desert sands in case it became necessary to escape through the deep desert. Once again armed guards and sentries are posted everywhere. Manson claimed these were to protect us but, as I've mentioned, the only time they

---

[101] "There were other surprises in the Brown report [a psychiatrist who examined Krenwinkel in Alabama]. Krenwinkel also told the doctor that she had fled to Mobile "because she was afraid of Manson finding her and killing her..." " (*Helter Skelter*, pg. 593)

A New Desperation

went out in force is when a Family member tried to escape.[102, 103, 104]

At the trial Vincent Bugliosi claimed that all the guns and supplies were to allow the Family to survive Helter Skelter. But the true reason for the preparations was clearly the police, not Helter Skelter. While Charles Manson still talked a lot about

---

[102] "Not long after this, Barbara [Hoyt] and another girl – Sherry Ann Cooper, aka Simi Valley Sherri – fled the Family's Death Valley hideout. Manson caught up with them in Ballarat, but, because other people were present, had let them go, even giving them twenty dollars for their bus fare to Los Angeles." [footnote] "We later received information indicating that Manson may have sent three of his followers to Los Angeles with instructions to either bring back the girls or kill them..." (*Helter Skelter*, pg. 221)

[103] "During the Barker raid, which took place over a three day period, two girls had appeared out of the bushes near a road some miles from the ranch, asking the officers for protection. They claimed they had been attempting to flee the "Family" and were afraid for their lives. One was named Stephanie Schram, the other Kitty Lutesinger." (*Helter Skelter*, pg. 101-102)

[104] "On the night of October 9... At about 4 A.M. as several of the officers [in the first Barker raid] were proceeding down one of the draws some distance from the ranch, they spotted two males asleep on the ground. Between them was a sawed-off shotgun. The two, Clem Tufts [t/n Steve Grogan] and Randy Morglea [t/n Hugh Rocky Todd], were placed under arrest. Though the officers were unaware of it, the pair had been stalking human game: Stephanie Schram and Kitty Lutesinger, two seventeen-year-old girls who fled the ranch the previous day." (*Helter Skelter*, pg. 170)

revolution and Armageddon in order to cover his true motives, he also gave lectures on how to kill with a knife... more specifically, how to kill police officers that came around the ranch.[105, 106] He wasn't preparing for a black/white race war at all.

And once again Charles Manson must have felt he had to cover up not only the true motive for the quick move and the change in the Family philosophy of love and acceptance, but for the bungling that took place in his murders. They *weren't* copy-cat murders now, they were supposed to throw fear into the establishment so they would leave us alone, or they

---

[105] "From Stephanie [Schram] I learned that while at Barker Manson had conducted a "murder school." He had given a Buck knife to each of the girls, and had demonstrated how they should 'slit the throats of pigs," by yanking the head back by the hair and drawing the knife from ear to ear. ... He also said they should "stab them in either ears or eyes and then wiggle the knife around to get as many vital organs as possible." ... Manson said that if the police pigs came to the desert, they should kill them, cut them in little pieces, boil the heads, then put the skulls and uniforms on posts, to frighten off others." (*Helter Skelter*, pg. 376 & 377)

[106] "...Things just seemed to get tighter and tighter. We had been undergoing constant indoctrination from Charlie on survival--on how to hide from the police, who from time to time were nosing around trying to find out what we were up to, and on how to maim and even kill. Quite a few of the kids with us had no knowledge of the murders already behind us. They still considered us a bunch of antiestablishment young people seeking a better world." (*Child of Satan, Child of God*, pg. 152)

were supposed to make the establishment stand up and take notice, or they were to start Helter Skelter, or to scare Terry Melcher, or to save the earth (I've never understood that one).

But the desert was hard and ugly. Maybe it was just that everyone in the Family felt hard and ugly on the inside. As I've said, all those directly involved in the murders were either in a state of shock or in hysterical overcompensation.[107, 108] Charles Manson's manipulations for drugs and power were falling apart. There were no drug connections in the desert. And his following was dwindling despite his armed guards. Those that were left were a tired and traumatized group who were ready to give up.

There was also no one to steal from in the desert. No one to con. Money was very limited, but Manson was afraid to go back to the city.

Luckily for everyone, our stay in the desert didn't last very long.

---

[107] [Prosecutor Vincent Bugliosi;] "She [Susan] was crazy. I had no doubt about it. Probably not legally insane, but crazy nonetheless." (*Helter Skelter*, pg. 230)

[108] "Q. "How did you feel [after the crimes], Linda?" A. "In a state of shock." " (*Helter Skelter*, pg. 355)

The Myth of Helter Skelter

Chapter 18

Last Daylight

When the police made their three day raid on Barker Ranch, where the Family stayed, they picked up the pathetic remains of Charles Manson's Family. It was the last free day Charles Manson ever had. He and about a dozen others, myself included, were put in jail originally, once again, for Grand Theft Auto. Eventually, once again, most were released.

I was not.

Someone had told the police that I knew something about a killing where someone's ear had been cut off. When the police told me I was under suspicion I thought Beausoleil had finally started to talk, trying to barter his way out of jail. Instead it was apparently one of the young girls who'd escaped from the desert hideout. Instead of being released with the others I was transferred to Los Angeles to be questioned about Gary Hinman's death.

The Myth of Helter Skelter

Chapter 19

Pretrial Jail Time

Most of what happened during this whole episode happened *after* I'd been arrested. In fact, after the bungling of the crimes – which covered a relatively short period of time – the wrangling and maneuvering and manipulation during the trial was where the real dramatics began. And that is where the myth of Helter Skelter began as well.

My own actions during this time have been misrepresented to such an extent that they have effectively buried me. Up until now there seemed little way of even attempting to lay out what really happened so that others could see it if they cared.

First it is important to note that everyone in the Family except for Bobby Beausoleil, Manson and myself had been set free. Watson had disappeared a week or so after the crimes even before we headed out to the desert. Linda Kasabian had run off, stealing a truck and abandoning her daughter in her escape. Leslie Van Houten, Patricia Krenwinkel, Bruce Davis,

The Myth of Helter Skelter

Catherine Share, Lynette Fromme and Sandra Good were all set free.

This left me basically on my own in County Jail. After several weeks I elicited the unwanted attention of two middle-aged career criminals,[109] Virginia Graham and Ronnie Howard, who apparently decided they were attracted to me. In order to avoid them I began talking about the biggest news on the Television – the killing of Sharon Tate.

Manson had spent much of his youth in correctional facilities, and during the growing paranoia after the crimes and into the desert he'd continually preached to us that when you're in jail you have to act tough in order to avoid getting targeted. You have to tell stories. You have to exaggerate to make yourself seem tougher and nastier than you are. So I exaggerated the only story I knew. I told them I knew who was responsible for the Tate crimes and, in fact, I knew who killed Sharon Tate. It was me.

I am not twenty-one years old anymore. Nor am I naive. I am quite aware that claiming I was merely

---

[109] "I was assigned a bunk opposite a tall, buxom woman named Ronnie, a pretty, but hardened former call girl in her thirties, who was charged with forging a prescription. Coming into 8000 with me that day was another call girl who had known Ronnie quite well. Her name was Virginia—a woman about my size and build, with short, reddish, curly hair. She had been picked up for parole violation." (*Child of Satan, Child of God*, pg. 158)

Pretrial Jail Time

lying to avoid unwanted homosexual advances in County Jail when I claimed to have killed Sharon Tate is very self-serving. And I am well aware the reader has no reason to believe me or to take my word for it.

And I don't want the reader to take my word for it. But then, I don't want the reader to take anyone else's word for it either.

Instead I merely offer the facts as told by others.

Manson has admitted he'd instructed everyone to act tough and tell stories in jail in order to survive if they were arrested. [110]

When the prosecutor, Vincent Bugliosi, asked these women why they hadn't contacted the police immediately if they knew I'd killed Sharon Tate, they both said they thought it obvious I had just been trying to act tough.[111, 112] It should be pointed out that even

---

[110] [Editor's Note: Manson tells this story in the book, *Manson, in his own words*, but I don't have the exact quote or page number. If anyone looks it up, please pass on the information to the publisher and it will be included in the updated version of the book.]

[111] "Virginia Graham thought she was sort of a "little girl lost," putting on a big act so no one would know now frightened she really was." (*Helter Skelter*, pg. 106)

[112] "Virginia [Graham] would later recall thinking, She's got to be kidding! She's making all this up. This is just too wild, too fantastic!"… "Ronnie [Howard] thought Sadie was "making it all up. She could have gotten it out of the papers."" (*Helter Skelter*, pg. 116)

the Prosecutor claimed these women weren't naïve, they were career criminals not likely to be fooled by a twenty-one year old girl. Their assessment was that I'd been lying.

Charles Watson also claimed I'd been lying when I said I killed Sharon Tate. He stated this in 1976,[113] and again in his own book, published in 1978.[114, 115]

---

[113] [Chaplain Ray recalling his 1975 conversation with Charles Watson, "I then remembered one of the reasons for my visit. "The last thing Susan Atkins said to me," I told Tex, "was that her hands had never taken a human life. You were there when the people at the Tate mansion were killed. You were there when the LaBiancas were murdered. Only you can tell me if Susan is telling the truth." "She's telling the truth," Tex Watson said. "She didn't kill anyone." (*God's Prison Gang*, Paperback version, pg. 35)

[114] "Later, Prosecutor Bugliosi - because of some things Susan-Sadie bragged about in jail in one of her attempts to get attention - was convinced that it was she who killed Sharon Tate, but his suspicion was not true." (*Will You Die For Me?*, paperback version pg. 137, hardback version, pg; 143)

[115] "She [Susan] exaggerated other things, however, such as claiming that she had stabbed Sharon... ... Later, Susan-Sadie herself told her story to the D.A.'s office and then to the grand jury (a more factual version that left out her claim to having stabbed Sharon Tate)..." (*Will You Die For Me?*, hardback version, pg; 161)

The District Attorney admitted that others in the family had told investigators I had not killed Sharon Tate as well.[116]

And finally, though I realize it doesn't hold any weight if you don't believe me anyway, I claimed this was a lie in 1975,[117] and again in my own book, published in 1977. This is also the story I told the Parole Board even earlier in the 1970's. I offer this merely to show you this isn't "Susan Atkins' New Version" of the crimes. If this is merely a self serving story of mine it is the same one I've been telling for over thirty years.[118] Even if you don't believe me, at least give me credit for having the intelligence to not change my story every three years.

---

[116] "And, contrary to what she had told the grand jury, she [Lake] knew a great deal. Tex, for example, had admitted to her that he'd stabbed Sharon Tate. He did it, he told her, because Charlie had ordered the killings." (*Helter Skelter*, pg. 276)

[117] "Now Susan turned her hands palms upward and said, much to my surprise: "I thank God that these two hands of mine have never taken a human life.""" (*God's Prison Gang*, Paperback version, pg. 29)

[118] [Susan's Note: After my 1996 Parole Board hearing one of the Newspapers announced boldly that I had "changed my story" and was "now claiming" I hadn't killed Sharon Tate. Since this is the same story I told the Grand Jury in 1969, it shows the extent to which the media doesn't research anything they print.]

That I was lying is further indicated by the fact that most of the other things I told the two women in jail have been proven to be lies.[119, 120]

The irony of the lie is that it had its desired effect. Both women avoided me from that point on. The down-side was that several weeks later I was "invited" to talk to the police about it.

The opportunity was a God-send. It had been impossible to sit in Jail with all that in my heart. I was going crazy. And the chance to get it out of me was a salvation in itself.[121]

---

[119] "Laughingly, she [Susan] told Ronnie [Howard] about some man whose head "we cut off," either out in the desert or in one of the canyons." (*Helter Skelter*, pg. 129)

[120] "One of the enduring Manson Family mysteries was cleared up by Grogan. It had become part of Manson Family lore, possibly to frighten all members who had mutinous thought, that Shea was decapitated by Grogan and had been cut up and buried in nine separate places at Spahn Ranch. ... Subsequently, Sergeant Gleason and his partner found Shea's remains in one piece at the spot designated by Grogan – the bottom of a steep embankment about a quarter mile down the road from the ranch." (*Helter Skelter*, AFTERWORD, pg. 509)

[121] "There was something mysterious about her [Susan]. She would talk rapidly for a few minutes, then pause, head slightly cocked to the side, as if sensing voices no one else could. ...She was crazy. I had no doubt about it. Probably not legally insane, but crazy nonetheless." Vincent Bugliosi (*Helter Skelter*, pg. 230)

Pretrial Jail Time

In hindsight it is interesting to point out that most people don't remember it was over two months after the crimes and both the Los Angeles Police Department and the Los Angeles Sheriff's Department had absolutely no leads. It is perhaps impossible now to look back and realize how odd, and frightening, it was for the entire community to have such a widely publicized crime with absolutely no leads.

It is with this backdrop that I suddenly told the LA District Attorney's office I knew exactly who was responsible for the crimes, that the Tate and LaBianca crimes were connected (something they still didn't realize), and that a suspect they'd questioned and already dismissed was actually the author of those crimes.

This revelation was such a bombshell that Vincent Bugliosi states in his account that without my testimony they had no case at all. Without my testimony they never would have been able to even indict Manson, let alone bring him to trial and convict him.[122, 123, 124, 125, 126]

---

[122] ""We don't even have a case to take to the grand jury," I [Bugliosi] told [LAPD Lieutenant] LaPage. "We're not even sure who the killers are or if they're free or in custody. All we have is a good lead [Susan's admission], but we're getting there."" (*Helter Skelter*, pg. 165)

[123] [Bugliosi, speaking of Susan's decision to testify] "...our whole case against Manson and the others rested on the decision of [Susan Atkins]." (*Helter Skelter*, pg. 214)

The Court appointed me a very conscientious Attorney named Richard Caballero. He told me to keep quiet and he'd make a deal with the Prosecutor. But I didn't care by that time. The nightmare was still in my heart and I had to let it out. In the end, despite my fears, I agreed to testify before the Grand Jury in order to indict Manson and the others responsible for the crimes. I didn't ask for any deal and I didn't ask for anything in exchange.[127] Despite the fact that without me there would be no case against Manson at

---

[124] "We can't get a grand jury indictment on this, I told him, adding "If Susan Atkins doesn't cooperate, we've had it."" (*Helter Skelter*, pg. 216)

[125] "Confidential Memo. From Deputy DA Vincent Bugliosi. To: District Attorney Evelle Younger. Subject: Status of Tate & LaBianca cases. The memo ran to thirteen pages, but the heart of it consisted of a single paragraph: "Without Susan Atkins' testimony on the Tate case, the evidence against two out of the five defendants [Manson and Kasabian] is rather anemic. Without her testimony on the LaBianca case, the evidence against five out of the six defendants [everyone except Van Houten] is non-existent." That was it. Without Sadie [Susan], we still didn't have a case." (*Helter Skelter*, pg. 283)

[126] "Without Susan Atkins, the prosecution had no case against Manson, and Manson knew it." (*Helter Skelter*, pg. 294)

[127] "Q [Bugliosi] Are you still willing to testify knowing that you are not being given immunity and you are not being freed of any of the charges that you may incriminate yourself about?

A [Atkins] I understand this... I just want to see [this] is taken care of." (Grand Jury Transcripts, pg. 9)

Pretrial Jail Time

all, I was the only person who didn't demand to have all charges against them dropped in exchange for agreeing to testify for the prosecution. I would be the only one to testify and still accept responsibility and go to trial for my part. [128, 129]

It is also worth pointing out that the public was putting an incredible amount of pressure on the Police and the District Attorney's office about this case. It was this public pressure that forced the District Attorney's Office to rush the case to the Grand Jury, and it's one of the reasons the myth of Helter Skelter was embraced before most of the facts of the case were uncovered.[130]

---

[128] [Susan's Note: In California a person has to be indicted by a Grand Jury before they can be charged and tried. In my case I'd agreed to testify against Manson and my co-defendants at the Grand Jury as long as I didn't have to testify in front of them at trial.]

[129] "Q   Are you freely willing to testify before the Grand Jury?
     A   Yes.
     Q   Now, do you understand that if you do testify that you may incriminate yourself?
     A   Yes, I do." (Grand Jury Transcripts, pgs. 8-9)

[130] "Susan Atkins would tell her story at the grand jury. We'd get an indictment. And that would be all we would have, a scrap of paper. For Caballero was convinced she would never testify at the trial. He was worried that even now she might suddenly change her mind. ...We had no choice but to rush the case to the grand jury, which was meeting the following day." (*Helter Skelter*, pg. 228)

Mr. Caballero set up a meeting with the Prosecutor. They explained to me they'd come to an agreement. I would testify at the Grand Jury but I wouldn't have to testify against Manson in open court. In addition I would be isolated and protected from my co-defendants while I was in jail. I would still be tried for my part in the crimes but my attorney had got the DA to agree they wouldn't seek the death penalty against me. The only stipulation was that I had to tell them the truth. If I didn't tell them the truth they could invalidate the whole deal, use my own testimony against me and I'd also face the Death Penalty.

So I sat down and told Mr. Bugliosi the truth. The interview was conducted in Mr. Caballero's office and lasted only two hours.[131]

But here's the problem. I had been implicated in the crimes because I'd told two women in jail I had killed Sharon Tate. That had been so shocking to them they had eventually contacted the police. Now I

---

[131] "Caballero drove me to his office in Beverly Hills. ... Susan Atkins was already there, having been taken out of Sybil Brand on the basis of another court order, requested by Aaron. ...my interview with Susan Atkins on the Tate-LaBianca murders was the first she had had with any law-enforcement officer. It would also be the last." (*Helter Skelter*, pg. 229)

was told I had to tell the police the truth or I'd be tried and executed. But the two were not the same.

So I told Mr. Bugliosi the truth. I hadn't killed Sharon Tate.

Years later, when he wrote his book about the crimes, Mr. Bugliosi stated he got the impression I was lying to him about this – he felt that I had, in fact, killed Sharon Tate.[132, 133]

I have to admit that during the time of the trials I did not like Mr. Bugliosi. It's hard to like someone who's part of a system that took your son away from you. And it's hard to like someone who knew how much pressure you'd been under and yet still told people you were a blood-drinking vampire, and who told you he'd have you executed if you didn't say and do what he wanted you to.

---

[132] "As on the tape, she admitted stabbing Frykowski but denied stabbing Sharon Tate. I'd conducted hundreds of interviews; you get a sort of visceral reaction when someone is lying. I felt she *had* stabbed Sharon but didn't want to admit it to me." (*Helter Skelter*, pg. 230)

[133] [Editor's Note: Though Mr. Bugliosi stated in his book that he believed Susan lied when she said she hadn't killed Sharon Tate, the fact that he presented her to the Grand Jury belies this claim. Under California law and the rules of professional ethics, it would have been both illegal and a violation of his professional duties for Mr. Bugliosi to have presented Susan's testimony to the Grand Jury if he believed it was not true.]

Mr. Bugliosi was wrong about a lot of things. And he was wrong about me killing Sharon Tate. But with the grace of God, and thirty-seven years of hindsight, I've come to respect the fact that as far as I know Mr. Bugliosi has always been careful to make it clear this is just his belief. This is what he *believes*. He doesn't claim to be God and he doesn't claim to *know* what happened that night.

Though this might sound like an odd point for me to stress, I assure you if you are ever unlucky enough to find yourself on trial there is a huge difference between a prosecutor who tells the jury he believes you did something you didn't and a prosecutor who tells the jury he *knows* you did something you didn't. It's a question of integrity.

Even though he's wrong about a lot of things, I've never caught Mr. Bugliosi deliberately lying about anything.

And so after the interview I was rushed to the Grand Jury. I told them what happened at the Cielo Dr. and LaBianca crimes. I told them the truth. Charles Manson was indicted and charged with the crimes. So were Linda Kasabian, Leslie Van Houten, Patricia Krenwinkel, and Charles Watson.

It took awhile for the police to find them all. Manson was still in jail but the others had scattered across the country. Some of them I did not even know by their real names.

Charles Watson was found in Texas. Patricia Krenwinkel in Alabama. Linda Kasabian had traveled to Salt lake City and then onward to New York. She turned herself in when she heard on TV that she'd been indicted.

And so I had it all out of my heart for the first time in months. I could breathe again. And I thought that was the end of it. We'd be tried and found guilty and that would be the end of it.

I was wrong.

The Myth of Helter Skelter

Chapter 20

The Pressure Inside

It is interesting to note that even at this late stage in the game Manson still believed he had a couple cards up his sleeve. As you will see, his manipulating and self interest didn't stop or falter for a moment. In the end I think you will see that ironically it was his own meddling in his case that cost him his freedom.

You must remember, Manson has prepared for this eventuality from the start. Every step of the way he had taken care to put distance between himself and the crimes he was organizing. Except for the Crowe blunder and his inability to keep from "showing how it's done" on the night of the LaBianca murders, he did pretty well at keeping himself covered. He'd also gone to great lengths to see that everyone who could possibly turn on him had their hands dirty as well.

Right away Charles Manson began to organize a network with which to run the Family from jail. Over the next couple years this network will be the means by which Charles Manson threatens witnesses, orders people to give and recant testimony, directs lawyers, orders jail-breaks, directs robberies, and even attempted murders.[134] Through members of the Family not charged with the crimes, namely Lynette Fromme and Sandra Good, Charles Manson began fabricating his defense.[135, 136]

And his defense primarily involved sacrificing everyone else to the flames.

His first defense was, of course, to deny any knowledge of the crimes. When I go to the Grand Jury and implicate him, his response is fast and brutal. My attorney, Richard Caballero receives death

---

[134] Share: "And I was programmed... I mean, I--we were sent notes constantly, "do this, do that, do the other thing." (Channel 2, Cover Story, 1993, KCBS, reporter: Harvey Levin.)

[135] "Some heavy scheming and a lot of communication had to be done. The police made both avenues possible when charges on several of the kids were dropped. With their release, I had the means to spread the word, "Clam up, no talking! Find out where the cops are getting their information." ...Lyn [Fromme] and Sandy [Good]... came to Independence and got an apartment. They were my eyes to everything that was going on. Though in jail some six or seven hours' drive from L.A. I had Lyn and Sandy burning up the highways and telephone lines with daily reports on who was saying what, and to whom. ..." (*Manson, in His Own Words*, pg. 220 & 221)

[136] "We were constantly visiting Charlie in prison, and we did everything on his orders." [Catherine Share] (National Examiner, May 24, 1994, pg. 11)

threats.[137] I receive visits from "friends" who suggest it might be in my own best interest for me to recant my testimony.[138, 139] I receive endless harassing letters. Threats to my life were posted around the jail.[140] And,

---

[137] "Beausoleil wasn't the only one being pressured. Without Susan Atkins, the prosecution had no case against Manson, and Manson knew it. Family members called Richard Caballero at all hours of the day and night. When cajoling didn't work, they tried threats." (*Helter Skelter*, pg. 294)

[138] "Always think of the Now... No time to look back... No time to say how." This rhyme was repeated in almost every letter Sandy, Squeaky, Gypsy, or Brenda sent to the defendants. Its meaning was obvious: Don't tell them anything. Through a barrage of letters, telegrams, and attempted visits, the Manson girls tried to get Beausoleil, Atkins, and Kasabian to dump their present attorneys, repudiate any incriminating statements they may have made, and engage in a united defense." (*Helter Skelter*, pg. 294)

[139] "When Manson again appeared before Judge Dell, on the twenty-eighth, he was still complaining about the limitations of his pro per privileges. For example, he wanted to interview Robert Beausoleil, Linda Kasabian, and Sadie Mae Glutz, but their attorneys had denied permission. Judge Dell informed him they had that right.
MANSON "I got a message from Sadie. She told me that the District Attorney had made her say what she had said." Manson was playing to the press, certain that they would pick up the charge, and they did. It was the next best thing to calling Susan on the phone and telling her how to recant." (*Helter Skelter*, pg. 291)

[140] "After Susan's story had appeared in the Los Angeles *Times*, little signs had appeared on the walls at Sybil Brand reading, "SADIE GLUTZ IS A SNITCH." This greatly upset

though I was supposed to be held incommunicado, Catherine Share gets herself arrested and put on my floor of the jail to scream and yell at me for a day and a half – I was a snitch, I was dead, Charlie wanted to see me, if I came back everything would be forgiven.[141]

And finally, I was reminded they could still find my son.

If one reads Mr. Bugliosi's account of the crimes there is something odd that doesn't pop out unless one is paying close attention. It is something that obviously didn't occur to Mr. Bugliosi.

My son had been taken by Social Services after I was arrested during the police raid at Spahn Ranch. So had Mary Brunner's son and Linda Kasabian's daughter. As I already mentioned, Linda Kasabian heard about the arrests and returned to Los Angeles to retrieve her daughter. She was horrified to hear from the Social Worker that a young woman claiming to be

---

Susan. And each time something like this happened, the scales seemed to tip a little more in Manson's favor." (*Helter Skelter*, pg. 294)

[141] "...I [Atkins] began to receive messages from Charlie through my visitors, the members of our group who were not in jail. He was working on me subtly, trying to bring me back under his domination, trying to get me to deny everything I had said. I eventually refused to testify at the trial, although I did go before the grand jury and tell every thing as accurately as l could remember it at that time." (*Child of Satan, Child of God*, pg. 163)

The Pressure Inside

Linda had showed up and tried to collect the child but had been turned away because she hadn't had any identification.[142]

Mary Brunner had been able to get her son back from Social Services when the Grand Theft Auto charges were dropped once she was released from jail. This is because Mary still had a driver's license.

But I didn't have a driver's license.

Mr. Bugliosi knows this. This is one of the reasons Linda was forced to drive to the Tate house – she was the only one who had a valid driver's license. (Mary Brunner was in jail at the time for using a stolen credit card.)

But when I was arrested again in the desert my son was taken into custody *again*. [143] Which means

---

[142] "[After she escaped Spahn Ranch] Linda did not talk to Charlie [on the phone], but she did talk to one of the other girls – she believed, but was not sure, it was Squeaky – who told her about the August 16 raid. The authorities had kept Tanya, she learned; she was now in a foster home. ...Linda subsequently called the Malibu police station and learned the name of the social worker who was handling Tanya's case." (continued)
[footnote] "On calling the social worker, Linda learned that another girl, passing as Tanya's mother, had attempted to reclaim Tanya a short time before. Though I couldn't prove it, I suspected that Manson had sent one of his girls to get Tanya, as insurance that Linda wouldn't talk." (*Helter Skelter*, pg. 390)

[143] "A total of ten females and three males were arrested during the first sweep of the Barker Ranch area. They ranged in age from sixteen to twenty-six, with the average nineteen or twenty. Two babies were also found: Zezozozse [sic?] Zadfrack

that although I didn't have any identification, Charles Manson made sure my son was retrieved and remained under his control.

This never occurred to the Prosecutor.

But this is important.

The way it happened is that Manson sent me to social services to find out where my son was. I then visited him several times at the home of the couple who were taking care of him. Despite the fact I still had no identification it was clear to them that he was my son. Then Manson had four men take me to visit my son one afternoon and after I left they brought me back in the evening prepared to steal my son away. But I found the window to his room wide open without a screen and him standing up in his crib looking toward the window as though waiting for me.

Over the years I have come to believe that the couple knew I was going to come back for him and they'd left the windows open like that on purpose.

But as soon as I got him I was ushered back into the car and driven back to Manson. My son was taken out of my hands and returned to where the other children were being kept "for his safety."[144]

Glutz, age one year, whose mother was Susan Atkins..." (*Helter Skelter*, pg. 170)

[144] [Editor's Note: This account differs slightly from the account in Susan's 1977 autobiography, where she claims it was Charles Watson and Sandra Goode who took her back to the

This isn't a breath-taking story, except that years later I'm still taunted by District Attorneys who imply I'm lying when I say I was threatened with the life of my son while I was in jail. They claim my son was safely in the care of the Social Services – no one could harm him. But if Manson had been able to find where my son was once he could find him again, and he could send people to get to him.

In the end, Manson's insistence that I recant my Grand Jury testimony shows a very naive understanding of the legal system. He believed that since my Grand Jury testimony was the only real evidence against him, if I recanted my testimony the charges would have to be dropped and he would have to be released.[145]

---

home. "Early one morning, close to two o'clock, Tex drove Sandra and me to the home. I left them in the car and went to the window of the baby's room, prepared to cut the screen and enter. But, oddly, the screen on the window was off, and the window open. I crawled into the room, and there was my baby. I have no explanation for it, but he was standing up in his crib, watching me enter. He merely stood, looking at me and smiling." (*Child of Satan, Child of God*, pg 150-151) When I asked her about it she said she definitely had visited earlier in the day and that one of the men Manson had sent with her to retrieve her son was Juan Flynn.]
[145] "Without Susan Atkins, the prosecution had no case against Manson, and Manson knew it." (*Helter Skelter*, pg. 294)

The Myth of Helter Skelter

I put up with this pressure for months. Through his minions, and then later in person, Charles Manson told me it would be "better for everyone," including myself and my son if I recanted my Grand Jury testimony. He said the DA had no real evidence against any of us and once I recanted my testimony we'd all be set free.[146]

Charles Manson's reasoning was clear – the only implication the District Attorney had on him was me. As for the claim that "we would *all* be set free," in truth, the only one who had any real evidence against them was me. Due to my talking to Virginia Graham and Ronnie Howard, if I recanted my testimony I would become the focal point of the DA's whole case. But this didn't matter to Charles Manson. For a man who insisted he loved his Family and would give his life for any of its members, he didn't seem to have any qualms about using my son to force me to let go of my one chance of avoiding the death penalty. And all just so he could beat a rap and not take responsibility for a crime I had already confessed to.

In the end I succumbed. But I have to point out the position I was in was not a very nice one. I was being promised by Manson that if I didn't do what he told me to I wouldn't live a year in prison and possibly

---

[146] "Now if the bitch [Atkins] will just retract her statement of, 'Charlie instructed us to,' there's no way these people are going to convict me of killing anyone." (*Manson, in His Own Words*, pg. 223)

The Pressure Inside

my son would be harmed as well.[147] On the other side I was being promised by the Prosecutor that if I didn't do what he told me to I would be executed.

In the end it became very clear. I'd seen what Charles Manson was capable of doing even to friends like Gary Hinman, and I knew he'd never considered me a "friend." I also knew Mr. Bugliosi still had to prove his case. In the spring of 1970 there was a real chance he might not be able to do this.[148, 149]

---

[147] [Susan's Note: This very real pressure was acknowledged by the Prosecutor in his account of the crimes when he spoke of Linda's tough decision to testify against Manson at trial, though he never acknowledged that I was under the same pressure; "Fleischmen [Linda's Attorney] wanted immunity for his client, yet from Linda's standpoint it would be better to be tried and acquitted than get immunity, testify against Manson and the others, and risk retribution by the Family." (*Helter Skelter*, pg. 295)]

[148] "[Patricia Krenwinkel's attorney Paul] Fitzgerald was not the only one who felt we had no case. The consensus in the DA's Office and the Los Angeles legal community ... was that the case against Manson and most of the other defendants would be thrown out on an 1118 motion. ...Some felt it wouldn't even get that far. *Newsweek* quoted an unnamed Los Angeles County deputy district attorney as saying that our case against Manson was so anemic that it would be thrown out even before we went to trial." (*Helter Skelter*, pg. 257)

[149] [February 6, 1970. Bugliosi still felt that the case against Manson was so weak that he asked the Inyo County DA's Office to re-file charges against Manson on arson.] "We were that afraid that Manson would be set free." (*Helter Skelter*, pg. 295)

I recanted my testimony.

In the thirty-six years that have followed this moment in my life I have been consistently vilified for my decision. The fact that I was the one who got Charles Manson indicted, and the fact that I was the one who told the Los Angeles Police Department he was even connected to the crimes, is regularly dismissed due to my recanting. At my parole hearings the District Attorney regularly asserts it shows my willing and deliberate commitment to Charles Manson. When I claim my recanting was the product of coercion and fear they usually scoff.

The truth is, Mr. Bugliosi himself claims to have been given up to three bodyguards during the trial,[150] and his family was moved into a "safe house" in response to threats against his life.[151, 152] He also

---

[150] "I [Bugliosi] now had three bodyguards, the judge a like number." (*Helter Skelter*, pg. 556)

[151] "...the few moments Gail, the kids, and I [Bugliosi] had together would be devoid of privacy, our home transformed into a fortress, a bodyguard not only living with us but accompanying me everywhere I went, following a threat by Charles Manson that he would 'kill Bugliosi.'" (*Helter Skelter*, pg. 160)

[152] "[judge] Older was already under protection. The next day the District Attorney's Office assigned me a body guard for the duration of the trial. Additional precautions were taken, which, since they're probably used in protecting others, needn't be enumerated, though one might be noted. In order to prevent a repetition of the events at 10050 Cielo Drive, a walkie-talkie

claims our judge was given three bodyguards, had a 24-hour guard on his home,[153] and carried a loaded gun under his judicial robes.[154] Both my Attorneys, Caballero as well as Shin, had their lives threatened.[155, 156] Patricia Krenwinkel's Attorney had his life threatened.[157] According to the Prosecutor, Leslie Van Houten's Attorney was actually killed at

---

was installed in our home, which provided instant communication with the nearest police station, in case the telephone wires were cut." (*Helter Skelter*, pg. 487)

[153] "Rumor had it that Judge Older himself had already received several threats. A secret memo he'd sent the sheriff, outlining courtroom security measures, ended with the following paragraph: "The sheriff shall provide the trial judge with a driver-bodyguard, and security shall be provided at the trial judge's residence on a 24-hour basis..."" (*Helter Skelter*, pg. 412)

[154] "From a reliable source, I learned that after the incident [Manson lunging at the judge] judge Older began wearing a .38 caliber revolver under his robes, both in court and in chambers." (*Helter Skelter*, pg. 502)

[155] "Family members called Richard Caballero [Susan's first attorney] at all hours of the day and night. When cajoling didn't work, they tried threats." (*Helter Skelter*, pg. 294)

[156] "...it was no secret that several, if not all, the defense attorneys were frightened of the Family. [Susan's second attorney] Daye Shinn, I was told by one of his fellows, kept a loaded gun in each room of his house, in case of an unannounced visitation." (*Helter Skelter*, pg. 487)

[157] "...[defense attorney] Fitzgerald made an interesting statement: "My life had been threatened three times, and I haven't come forward and talked about it."" (*Helter Skelter*, pg. 496)

The Myth of Helter Skelter

Manson's command.[158, 159] And all of this was while Manson was locked away in jail.

Most of the Family members were still free at that time. This included Lynette Fromme and Sandra Good, whom the Prosecutor claimed followed him around with a knife,[160, 161] as well as Bruce Davis and Steve Grogan both of whom would eventually be

---

[158] "Before his disappearance, Ronald Hughes, the missing defense attorney in the Tate-LaBianca murder trial, confided to close friends that he was in fear of Manson." Los Angeles *Times* (*Helter Skelter*, pg. 521)

[159] "One thing is now known, however. If an admission by one of Manson's most hard-core followers is correct, Ronald Hughes *was* murdered by the Manson Family." (*Helter Skelter*, pg. 651)

[160] "And several times when I left the Hall of Justice at night, I was followed by various Family members, including Sandy. Only the first time disturbed me. Gail and the kids were circling the block in our car, and I was afraid they would be identified or the license number spotted. When I pretended not to see her, Gail quickly sized up the situation and drove around until I was able to shake my "followers," though, as she later admitted to me, she was far less cool than she appeared." (*Helter Skelter*, pg. 487)

[161] [Editor's Note: there is an incident recalled by Vincent Bugliosi in *Helter Skelter*, in which Sandra Goode and some male followers of Charles Manson followed him around with knives until he turned around and confronted them. I don't have the page number or the quote. If anyone can locate them, please send the information to the publisher and it will be included in the next copy of the book.]

The Pressure Inside

convicted and recommended for death by their juries.[162]

There were very real reasons to fear Charles Manson even while he was incarcerated. And the District Attorney's Office knew this.[163, 164, 165, 166]

---

[162] "[Potential witnesses] needed only to pick up a newspaper or turn on TV to see that many of the Family members were still roaming the streets; that Steve Grogan, aka Clem, was out on bail, while the Inyo County grand theft charges against Bruce Davis had been dismissed for lack of evidence. Neither Grogan, Davis, nor any of the others suspected of beheading Shorty Shea had been charged with that murder, there being as yet no physical proof that Shea was dead." (*Helter Skelter*, pg. 341)

[163] "Q. "... Now, how scared of Manson are you?" [The Los Angeles Sheriff's Office asked Danny DeCarlo when it appeared he was afraid to testify against Manson.] A. [DeCarlo] "I'm scared shitless. I'm petrified of him. He wouldn't hesitate for a second. If it takes him ten years, he'd find that little boy of mine and carve him to pieces." Q. "You give that motherfucker more credit than he deserves. If you think Manson is some kind of god that is going to break out of jail and come back and murder everybody that testifies against him -" But it was obvious DeCarlo didn't put that past Manson. Even if he remained in jail, there were the others." (*Helter Skelter*, pg. 152)

[164] "One of our witnesses, Barbara Hoyt, has left her parent's home. I don't have all the details, but the mother said Barbara received a threat on her life, that if she testified at this trial she would be killed and so will her family." (*Helter Skelter*, pg. 471)

[165] "Ouisch also confided [to Hoyt] that Linda Kasabian was not long for this world; at most she had six months to live." (*Helter Skelter*, pg. 474)

The Myth of Helter Skelter

---

[166] [Editor's Note: The book Helter Skelter contains comments about roughly 25 people who claimed to have been in fear for their lives from Manson prior to his arrest. The book also contains comments about roughly 75 people who claimed to have been in fear for their lives from Manson *after* he'd been arrested and while he was in jail.]

Chapter 21

Being Thrown Away by Both Sides

I recanted my testimony and immediately heard that despite Manson's assurances we'd all be freed, instead the District Attorney merely made a new deal with Linda Kasabian.[167] Now *she* was going to be their "evidence." I was still going to face trial, but now I was going to face the death penalty too.

But suddenly it became very clear. I'd been promised not merely immunity from the death penalty, I'd been promised protection and isolation from my co-defendants. The District Attorney knew I was receiving visits from known Family members while supposedly being held incommunicado.[168] And he

---

[167] "Caballero told Aaron and me that it looked as if we'd lost our star witness [Susan]. We contacted Gary Fleischman, Linda Kasabian's attorney, and told him we were ready to talk." (*Helter Skelter*, pg. 341)

[168] "Or perhaps it was simply that the numerous messages Manson was sending, by other Family members, were getting to [Susan]." (*Helter Skelter*, pg. 341)

knew Catherine Share had been placed on my floor and on my hall of the Los Angeles County Jail (which had four floors of jail cells) and that she was allowed to yell threats down at me for the better part of two days.[169] They knew threatening signs were being found hung on the walls of the jail, indicating I was a snitch, and they knew this was pushing me closer and closer to recanting.[170]

In hindsight I've come to believe this is exactly what the prosecution wanted.[171] And there are several good reasons for this belief.

In California you can't use the testimony of one defendant against their co-defendants unless there is some corroborating evidence. That means you have to have at least one other piece of evidence to indicate

---

[169] [Editor's Note: This incident is documented somewhere but I do not have the page or the quote. If anyone finds it, please pass the information on to the publisher and it will be included in the next edition.]

[170] "After Susan's story had appeared in the Los Angeles *Times*, little signs had appeared on the walls at Sybil Brand reading, "SADIE GLUTZ IS A SNITCH." This greatly upset Susan. And each time something like this happened, the scales seemed to tip a little more in Manson's favor." (*Helter Skelter*, pg. 294)

[171] "Given a choice between Susan and Linda as the star witness for the prosecution, I much preferred Linda… But in the rush to get the case to the grand jury, we'd made the deal with Susan and, like it or not, we were stuck with it. Unless Susan bolted." (*Helter Skelter*, pg. 295)

the testimony of the codefendant is truthful. In my case, though I was the one responsible for Charles Manson being indicted and charged, and though I was the one who told the District Attorney's Office what happened and who was involved, my testimony could only go so far at trial.

My testimony could be used against Charles Watson and Patricia Krenwinkel because the police had found a fingerprint from both of them at the crime scene. And Leslie Van Houten had spoken to another girl at the Ranch about the LaBianca crime. Charles Manson himself had made several vaguely incriminating remarks to various people indicating his connection to the crimes. This provided the corroborating evidence that would allow my testimony to be used against them.

But the Prosecutor had no corroborating evidence against Linda Kasabian. This meant he wouldn't be able to use my testimony against her and he didn't have anything else.[172, 173]

---

[172] "... without Susan's testimony we had no evidence against Linda, ..." (*Helter Skelter*, pg. 295)

[173] [Note: There actually was corroborating evidence against Linda Kasabian because she'd told people in Salt Lake City about her involvement in the crime, but since none of these people ever came forward the Prosecutor never found out about them until after he'd already made the deal with Linda. (This fact is documented by Vincent Bugliosi in *Helter Skelter*, but I do not have the page or the quote. If anyone find this information, please send it to the publisher and it will be included in the next edition.)]

In the end it was obvious the District Attorney would rather have made a deal with Linda from the start – they believed they weren't going to be able to prosecute her anyway — but unfortunately for the DA Linda hadn't come forward until she'd been indicted.

I, on the other hand, was different. If I could be induced to recant my testimony, and therefore invalidate my deal, what I'd said to the women in County Jail could be used as corroborating evidence for anything Linda said against me. [174, 175]

Vincent Bugliosi admitted to being angered when he found the DA's office had offered me a deal.[176] Why? Because he was horrified by my participation in the crimes? No. Because from the DA's point of view I was the only one he felt he had a

---

[174] "But in the rush to get the case to the grand jury, we'd made the deal with Susan and, like it or not, we were stuck with it. Unless Susan bolted." (*Helter Skelter*, pg. 295)

[175] "Now if Susan bolts back to Charlie," I [Prosecutor Vincent Bugliosi] told Aaron, "and we're left without a major witness for the trial – as well we might be – then we can talk about a deal for Linda. In fact, if that happens, Linda may be our only hope." (*Helter Skelter*, pg. 250)

[176] "I was in total disagreement. "If what she told Ronnie Howard is true, Atkins personally stabbed to death Sharon Tate, Gary Hinman, and who knows how many others! *We don't give that gal anything*! ...as a last resort – a very, very last resort – we can turn to Atkins." (*Helter Skelter*, pg. 165, emphasis in original.)

good chance of prosecuting thanks to my statements to Virginia Graham and Ronnie Howard. He would much rather have chosen Linda, against whom he had *no* corroborating evidence, as the one he'd have offered immunity to.

From a prosecutorial point of view it just made sense to try to get rid of me.

When I finally did recant my testimony, Manson's first question to me was "have you gotten to Linda?" His foremost interest was still himself.

But unlike me, Linda Kasabian couldn't be threatened. Manson couldn't get to her daughter — she was with Linda's family. And Manson couldn't threaten Linda with harm once she got to prison — unlike me Linda had demanded complete immunity in return for testifying, meaning she wouldn't even be tried for the crimes and would never go to prison for her part in them.

Also unlike me, she was being given real protection and isolation from her co-defendants. An indication of how the District Attorney's Office could have prevented me from suffering the pressures I did when they left me in the jail is seen in how differently they handled Linda Kasabian – the Prosecutor himself went straight over to the jail the very day he made the deal with Linda and talked to the Sheriff in charge and had her put in isolation. [177, 178, 179] True isolation. On a separate floor from all the other people in jail. And he kept her there for the entire trial.[180]

This makes the fact they left me in the main jail population even though they knew I was being threatened and pressured a good indicator they knew what they were doing. They knew I was being pushed closer and closer to recanting.

Another indicator the District Attorney's Office wasn't being entirely honest with me is the fact that

---

[177] [Editor's Note: The account of Vincent Bugliosi going straight to the jail to talk to the Sheriff in person is contained somewhere in *Helter Skelter*, but I do not have the page or the quote. If anyone finds this information, please send it to the publisher and it will be included in the next edition.]

[178] "Until her baby was born, Linda was being kept in an isolated cell off the infirmary. She had no contact with the other inmates... After the baby was born, however, she would be reassigned to one of the open dormitories... I made a note to talk to Captain Carpenter to see if other arrangements could be made." (*Helter Skelter*, pg. 358)

[179] "In the interim I had talked to Captain Carpenter, and he had agreed to let Linda remain in her former cell just off the infirmary. I checked it out myself. It was a small room... It was clean but bleak. Far more important, it was safe." (*Helter Skelter*, pg. 360)

[180] "She [Kasabian] had been in custody since December 3, 1969. Unlike Manson, Atkins, Krenwinkel, and Van Houten, she had been in solitary confinement the whole time." (*Helter Skelter*, pg. 447-448)

they only interviewed me once for two hours.[181] They later claimed my deal would have been invalidated even if I hadn't recanted simply because I had not been "entirely truthful" with them. When they clarified what "not entirely truthful" meant they claimed I hadn't told them Manson had taken Linda Kasabian, Steve Grogan and me out to Venice Beach after the LaBianca's and ordered us to kill a friend of Linda's.

The truth is I hadn't told the prosecutor about that event because the interview never touched on it. The prosecutor was the one asking the questions and he never asked about it. Compared to the issues he was talking to me about it didn't seem relevant, especially as we hadn't done it. And the Prosecutor only talked to me for two hours — it never came up.

The Prosecutor's claim that I had deliberately omitted this is highly suspect, and I think he knows that.[182]

---

[181] "Although she had opened up to both Virginia Graham and Ronnie Howard, my interview with Susan Atkins on the Tate-LaBianca murders was the first she had had with any law-enforcement officer. It would also be the last." (*Helter Skelter*, pg. 229)

[182] "Like the church and sports-car incidents, Susan Atkins had not mentioned the Venice incident to me, nor had she said anything about it when testifying before the grand jury. While I felt that she might have forgotten the two earlier incidents, I suspected the third was omitted intentionally, since it directly involved her as a willing partner in still another attempted murder. It was possible, however, that had I had more time to

Mr. Bugliosi himself confesses he *rarely* interviews witnesses just once, usually going back to talk to them four or five times, because they often overlook things they remember later.[183, 184, 185, 186] This indicates he knew perfectly well if he only interviewed me once there was a very good chance he could find something we hadn't covered. Then he could use that to claim I was "not entirely truthful" and use that to invalidate my deal.

In contrast, as soon as he made a deal with Linda he started interviewing her regularly. He claims

---

interview Susan, that too might have come out." (*Helter Skelter*, pg. 367)

[183] "I rarely interviewed a witness just once. Often the fourth or fifth interview will bring out something previously forgotten or deemed insignificant, which, in proper context, may prove vital to my case." (*Helter Skelter*, pg. 299)

[184] "I had no idea how often the police had interviewed Winifred Chapman, the Polanski's maid. I'd talked to her a number of times myself before I realized there was one question so obvious we'd all overlooked it." (*Helter Skelter*, pg. 371)

[185] "...it occurred to me [Bugliosi] that [Susan] might had made incriminating statements to others, so I asked LAPD to locate any girls Atkins had been particularly close to at Sybil Brand. ... Not until the fifth or sixth time I interviewed her did Roseanne recall a conversation which, though it seemed unimportant to her, I found very significant." (*Helter Skelter*, pg. 388)

[186] "This was to be the start of a pattern. Having questioned each of the witnesses not once but a number of times, I had uncovered a great deal of information not previously related to the police..." (*Helter Skelter*, pg. 427)

to have spent as many as fifty hours interviewing her, some of these interviews lasting up to nine hours. In addition he gave her a pad of paper and told her to write down anything she'd overlooked when they'd talked. He claims some of the letters she wrote him were ten or more pages long. [187] In fact even minor witnesses were interviewed for hours and hours. [188, 189]

---

[187] "I talked to her [Kasabian] from 1 to 4:30 P.M. on the twenty-eighth [February 1970]. It was the first of many long interviews, a half dozen of them lasting six to nine hours... At the end of each interview I'd tell her that if, back in her cell, anything occurred to her which we hadn't discussed, to "jot it down." A number of these notes became letters to me, running to a dozen or more pages. ...The more times a witness tells his story, the more opportunities there are for discrepancies and contradictions, which the opposing side can then use for impeachment purposes. While some attorneys try to hold interviews and pre-trial statements to a minimum so as to avoid such problems, my attitude is the exact opposite. If a witness is lying, I want to know it before he ever takes the stand. In the more than fifty hours I spent interviewing Linda Kasabian, I found her, like any witness, unsure in some details, confused about others, but never once did I catch her even attempting to lie." (*Helter Skelter*, pg. 343-344)

[188] "I [Bugliosi] spent many hours interviewing Stephanie Schram [a minor witness in the case]..." (*Helter Skelter*, pg. 376)

[189] "In interviewing Dianne [Lake][another minor witness], I learned a number of things which hadn't come out in her earlier interviews. ...The interview lasted several hours." (*Helter Skelter*, pg. 403)

I was the witness Mr. Bugliosi claimed without which they "had no case at all," and yet he interviewed me only once. And for only two hours. And then he claimed I hadn't told him "everything."

Another interesting quirk about the DA's decision to get me to recant is that they now didn't have anyone to testify about the Hinman case either. So they not only had to give Linda Kasabian complete immunity for her part in the seven Cielo/LaBianca killings, they now had to make a deal with Mary Brunner to get her to testify against Bobby Beausoleil about Gary Hinman's killing. Following Linda's example, Mary Brunner demanded and had to be given complete immunity for her part in Gary's death.

It's worth pointing out that in the end I was the only person who agreed to testify against Manson without demanding complete immunity. Everyone else who had anything over them demanded complete immunity. From Linda Kasabian[190] to Ronnie Howard and Virginia Graham. From Danny DeCarlo[191] to

---

[190] "On Monday, August 10, 1970, the People petitioned the Court for immunity for Linda Kasabian. Though Judge Older signed the petition the same day, it was not until the thirteenth that he formally dropped all charges against her and she was released." (*Helter Skelter*, pg. 447)

[191] "It was agreed that if DeCarlo testified in the Beausoleil trial, LASO would drop the motorcycle engine theft charge against him." (*Helter Skelter*, pg. 164)

Being Thrown Away by Both Sides

Mary Brunner.[192] I was the only one who testified about my part in the crimes and still accepted responsibility for them.[193]

But this is not an indictment of Linda. Linda did what she should have done.[194] But she had a lot of advantages that I did not. Her daughter was now in the hands of her family on the east coast. She was being held incommunicado. *True* incommunicado. No one was allowed to see her. No one was allowed to talk to her... for nine long months.

Charles Manson had made another incredible blunder. If he had left me as the DA's main witness he would have been able to continue to threaten me with my son and undermine the prosecution's attack. Now there was no way for him to touch the DA's main witness.

But his goal was obvious. With my testimony recanted, he immediately called for a dismissal of the

---

[192] "[Mary] Brunner was given complete immunity in exchange for her testimony [at Beausoleil's second trial]." (*Helter Skelter*, pg. 395)

[193] "In accordance with the earlier discussion between our office and LAPD, we said that if Susan would cooperate with us, we would probably let her plead guilty to second degree murder – i.e. we would not seek the death sentence, but we would ask for life imprisonment." (*Helter Skelter*, pg. 214)

[194] "On questioning, the defendant [Susan] stated... She does not hold Linda [Kasabian's] position in the prosecution against her..." (Probation Officer's Report, 4-19-71)

charges against him. That I was still implicated by my talking to Virginia Graham and Ronnie Howard, and therefore now faced eight counts of first-degree murder and the death penalty, didn't bother him at all. I was disposable.

And suddenly I realized I'd been thrown away by the DA's Office at the point when I was no longer useful to them, and I was being thrown away by Manson now that I was no longer needed by him.

Neither side had ever wanted me.

Chapter 22

The Selling of Bobby Beausoleil

Bobby Beausoleil's first trial had ended in a hung jury. But the investigation into the Cielo-LaBianca murders was still turning up more evidence and more people who knew about the death of Gary. Mary Brunner was identified and charged as a co-defendant for the murder of Gary Hinman. Manson must have began to suspect that Beausoleil was thinking of making a deal; Manson decided to throw Bobby to the wolves.

Mary Brunner was told to make a deal with the DA's office. At Bobby Beausoleil's second trial Mary insisted that Bobby had acted on his own, that no one had prompted his killing of Gary Hinman.[195] Bobby must have realized what was happening — his "brother" Charles Manson was stabbing him in the back. In response Bobby took the stand himself and

---

[195] "Chief witness for the prosecution [at Beausoleil's second trial] was Mary Brunner ... who testified that she had witnessed Beausoleil stab Hinman to death." (*Helter Skelter*, pg. 395)

declared that Manson was responsible for the murder. This is exactly what Manson had feared Beausoleil would do from the beginning, and it was exactly what he didn't need right now. But it was too late for Beausoleil. He was convicted of first-degree murder.

Charles Manson had orchestrated the killing of Gary Hinman perfectly. By the time Beausoleil realized he was being thrown to the wolves his credibility was destroyed and he couldn't even finger Manson convincingly.

But Manson was still afraid of being fingered for Crowe, the only murder he didn't think he could worm his way out of. And so he immediately sent Mary Brunner back to recant her testimony in order to pacify Bobby. Then Bobby Beausoleil moved for a mistrial and release, claiming Mary's testimony was the only evidence against him.[196] He was denied. And Manson was left to worry about whether

---

[196] "In court to petition for a new trial, Bobby Beausoleil produced an affidavit, signed by Mary Brunner, stating that her testimony in his trial "was not true," ...Investigating further, Burt [Katz, prosecutor] learned that a few days before she was due to testify, Mary Brunner had been visited by Squeaky and Brenda at her parents' home in Wisconsin. She was again visited by Squeaky, this time accompanied by Sandy, two days before she signed the affidavit. Burt charged that the girls, representing Manson, had coerced Mary Brunner into repudiating her testimony." (*Helter Skelter*, pg. 397)

The Selling of Bobby Beausoleil

Beausoleil would turn to the DA's office about the Crowe incident.

So far in the investigation of the Cielo /LaBianca murders, the DA Vincent Bugliosi was digging as deep as he could for a motive and finding nothing but talk of revolution, environmentalism, and Helter Skelter.

Charles Manson must have smiled.

There was nothing about Bernard Crowe. All that nonsense Manson had been spewing for months had paid off. All the stupid people who had trusted him to lead them were so confused as to what the murders were actually about that Bugliosi was getting nothing but nonsense. Charles Manson knew he couldn't possibly be convicted on that. No one would believe that. No one would believe he had tried to instigate a race war to gain control of the world. And once a jury scoffed at that, Manson would simply show there was no proof he was at Gary Hinman's house or the Cielo Dr. residence, and he'd left the LaBianca residence before anyone was hurt. He was in the clear.

To this end he continued to actively uphold the Helter Skelter motive himself. In interviews with the press Manson spoke of revolution, society's ills, and the need to call the attention of the whole world. He instructed Lynette Fromme and Sandra Good and the members of the Family still free to stir the media up with claims that the murders were symbolic acts of revenge for the destruction of the planet. The girls who held vigil outside the courthouse were instructed to fill the newspapers with threats of impending doom and retaliation if he, Manson, was convicted. In the end, Manson believed, he would insist it was the girls' ridiculous ideas that had prompted the killings and he had nothing to do with any of it, and he would slip away and leave us to die.

Manson must have smiled.

But he was missing something. His lust for media attention and his iron-clad control of his codefendants' legal representation was beginning to show through. He didn't realize, but the jury was beginning to see the extent of his control and manipulation of the Family. And the bizarre courtroom antics he arranged to make my codefendants and me look crazy and wild were beginning to back-fire as the jury and the press slowly became convinced the Family was just crazy enough to actually believe in Helter Skelter. Perhaps the murders *were* committed due solely upon the deranged delusions of a madman.

It must be mentioned that in the fall of 1969, at the time of his arraignment for the Cielo/LaBianca murders, Charles Manson was almost universally believed by the professional and legal communities to be either completely innocent of the crimes or in a position that he could never be successfully prosecuted for them.[197, 198] And this was probably true. There was no physical evidence or sound motive connecting Charles Manson to the crimes. What eventually put Charles Manson on death row was his own foolish interruption of his legal defense.

If, from the start, he had just let his State-appointed lawyers do their jobs he probably would not have ended up in prison... that is, until he got caught for something else. But his involvement with his own legal representation not only confounded and undermined his lawyers, it made his controlling and manipulating nature more and more obvious.

Toward the end of the guilt phase of the trial it began to look as though the jury, and certainly the press, might actually be taking the Helter Skelter motive seriously. But Charles Manson was so wound up in the media blitz and being the center of attention, he didn't even notice his twilight was coming.

---

[197] The consensus in the DA's Office and the Los Angeles legal community ... was that the case against Manson and most of the other defendants would be thrown out on an 1118 motion. ...Some felt it wouldn't even get that far. *Newsweek* quoted an unnamed Los Angeles County deputy district attorney as saying that our case against Manson was so anemic that it would be thrown out even before we went to trial." (*Helter Skelter*, pg. 257)

[198] [February 6, 1970. Bugliosi still felt that the case against Manson was so weak that he asked the Inyo County DA's Office to re-file charges against Manson on arson.] "We were that afraid that Manson would be set free." (*Helter Skelter*, pg. 295)

The Myth of Helter Skelter

Chapter 23

And the Heavens Cried

Sometime toward the end of the guilt phase of the trial something occurred which only merited a minor note from prosecuting attorney Vincent Bugliosi. The fact that Vincent Bugliosi didn't realize the true significance of this occurrence shows his lack of understanding of the crimes.

While being escorted between jail and court it is reported that Charles Manson was led down one of the halls of the justice building when he met another prisoner being led in the other direction. It was Bernard Crowe.

Vincent Bugliosi reported that the sheriffs escorting Manson said he turned to Crowe and said, "Sorry I had to do it, but you know how it is."[199] (This

---

[199] "...As he [Crowe] was being escorted down the hall, he passed Manson and his guard, who were on their way back from the attorney room. Charlie did a quick about-face, then told Crowe, according to the deputies who were present, "Sorry I had to do it, but you know how it is." Crowe's response, if there was one, went unreported." (*Helter Skelter*, pg. 381)

exchange alone, if true, undermines Manson's claim that the shooting was in self defense — no apology would have been necessary.)

The true irony of this moment can only be appreciated if one understands the real reason all the killings began – to get money so Manson could run away from the police and the Black Panthers, who he was sure were coming after him for killing Bernard Crowe.

At this one moment it must have all became obvious to Charles Manson. Bernard Crowe wasn't dead. Manson hadn't killed anyone that day. What's worse, it must have been immediately obvious to Manson that Bernard Crowe had never mentioned the shooting to the police. And none of Crowe's friends had either. And no Panthers had ever gone up to wipe out Spahn Ranch. Bernard Crowe must not even know any Panthers!

That was the moment when the true horror and tragedy of all those murders should have come to Manson. That was the moment it became obvious that when Charles Manson had ordered the murder of Gary Hinman no one, not the police or the Panthers, was pursuing him. There had been no need for desperation. There had been no need for money to flee. And there had been no need for Gary Hinman to die.

So, Charles Manson's fears about Crowe led to the completely unnecessary murder of Gary Hinman. Bobby Beausoleil's arrest for the murder of Gary led to the horrific murders at the Cielo Dr. residence and the LaBianca residence. The murders at the Cielo Dr. and LaBianca residences led, ultimately, to the murder of Donald Shea. And all of it was for nothing!

Seeing Bernard Crowe alive and in police custody should have sent a sickening chill through Charles Manson. The horror of nine innocent people dead should have filled him.

But I don't know if it did. What I really think troubled him was the thought that Crowe might press charges or put a hit out on him.

On a personal note, I have often wished I could have been there when this exchange took place. To see the look on Charles Manson's face at the moment when he realized nine people had died and eight more were on their way to death row *for nothing*. All for nothing.

I would have liked to have seen if even a flicker of recognition of that horror showed on his face for even a second — some sign that for one moment in his life he actually cared about those people.

And the heavens must have cried.

The Myth of Helter Skelter

Chapter 24

The Lies that Bind

Toward the end of the guilt phase of the trial Manson should have realized things weren't going well. He'd tied his lawyers' hands and insisted on controlling everything they did in court, even though he knew nothing about the law or legal proceedings, and he'd foiled their every attempt to help him.[200] And this was despite the fact that, nine months ago, ninety percent of the legal community believed there would be no way to convict Manson.[201] But those people had underestimated Charles Manson's need to control everyone around him even when he didn't know what he was doing.

---

[200] "Manson's goal: to run the entire defense himself. In court as well as out, Charlie intended to retain complete control of the Family." (*Helter Skelter*, pg. 269)

[201] "But it was something more. You got the feeling that despite his verbal utterances, Manson was convinced that he was going to beat the rap. ... The problem, at years end [1969], was that there was a very good chance that ... Manson would be right." (*Helter Skelter*, pg. 279)

At the end of the guilt phase of the trial Charles Manson got the shock of his life when he found out he'd actually been convicted for the murders of the seven people at the Cielo Dr. and LaBianca residences. And he'd thought he'd been so careful to distance himself from the murders. The immaturity of his knowledge about the law can be seen in his lack of understanding that just his knowledge that the murders were going to take place and his efforts to cover them up afterwards, even without the fact that he'd orchestrated them, made him an accessory to the murders and therefore legally culpable. The fact that he'd helped tie up the LaBiancas made his part in the murders active and premeditated. So he shouldn't have been surprised.

But to someone who thought he was the only one who mattered in the world this blow must have been tremendous. And he'd been convicted with that ridiculous nonsense about Helter Skelter at that!

Chapter 25

The Penalty Plan

Having been convicted, Manson changed his strategy going into the penalty phase of the trial.

In California a guilty verdict during the guilt phase of the trial is followed by a penalty phase, where the jury determines the penalty imposed. In the case of First Degree Murder in 1969, the choice was between seven-years-to-life in prison or the death penalty.

During the trial Manson had been careful to tie the hands of his co-defendants. He had forced each of us to fire our court-appointed attorneys and to hire attorneys who had solicited Manson.[202] The result

---

[202] "Only later would we learn what was happening behind the scenes. Manson had set up his own communications network. Whenever he heard that an attorney for one of the girls had initiated a move on behalf of his client which could conceivably run counter to Manson's own defense, within days that attorney would be removed from the case....Manson's goal: to run the

was that Manson had four attorneys and my co-defendants and I had none.[203]

This meant that during the trial Manson had prevented any of us from putting forth a defense. The reason is obvious. What could our attorneys have said other than, "These young women were forced into the crimes by the machete-wielding maniac Charles Manson"? Charles Manson's hopes of being found not guilty rested squarely on me and my co-defendants taking the full weight of responsibility for the crimes. He didn't want us to have a defense. We were expendable. We were slated to die.[204]

But having been found guilty, Manson had to totally overhaul his strategy. He was now already implicated in the Hinman murder, so hiding the copy cat motive was no longer necessary. He also now knew he hadn't killed Bernard Crowe, so he didn't have to worry about the police finding out about that. He now believed his best bet lay in throwing doubt upon the Helter Skelter motive he'd originally been so happy to see the prosecution latch onto. He'd also

---

entire defense himself. In court as well as out, Charlie intended to retain complete control of the Family." (*Helter Skelter*, pg. 269)

[203] "He [Manson] had succeeded in forming a unified defense team. Although Fitzgerald remained its nominal head, it was obvious who was calling the shots." (*Helter Skelter*, pg. 418)

[204] "...Manson had told Springer: "No matter what happens, the girls will take the rap for it."" (*Helter Skelter*, pg. 338)

The Penalty Plan

take every opportunity to try to slander the prosecution's main witness, Linda Kasabian.

This is one of the reasons why my case is so strange. It was handled completely backwards. Our defense lawyers put forth no defense during the trial and then the entire defense was laid out during the penalty phase. This is one of the reason why, thirty-seven years later, no matter what I say skeptics can claim, "nothing like this was ever brought out at the trial." And they're entirely correct – because *no defense was brought out at the trial.*

So this was the new plan Manson unfolded for the penalty phase. It was based on one of the most elementary manipulative tricks of them all — mix your lies with a lot of truth.

The copy cat motive would be uncovered and admitted, but with a few novel changes that would suit Charles Manson. First and foremost, the defense would claim Manson didn't have anything to do with the planning of the murders. The man who told people in the Family what to wear, how to cut their hair, and broke chairs over people's heads if they talked when he didn't want them to, was now to be portrayed as an innocent bystander to the most all-encompassing decision ever made by the Family. A completely ridiculous story to anyone who'd ever been in the Family or even seen the Family – but would the jury buy it?

The second most important change was that Linda Kasabian would be portrayed as the main ring-leader in the murders. This would help discredit her as a witness against Manson and give the illusion she was fingering Manson just to remove herself from the picture as much as possible. Once again, to anyone who knew the Family or Linda Kasabian the charge was ridiculous.

It should be pointed out that Linda Kasabian was not the angel Vincent Bugliosi claimed she was. (She was the only one besides Charles Manson himself to drive the Family to the crime scenes, and she was the only one to hide the weapons after the Cielo Dr. crimes.) But she was certainly not responsible or culpable in any way for the murders. She was just as frightened and unwilling as the rest of us (during the Cielo Dr. murders she actually ran away, and the next night she deliberately steered Charles Manson away from potential victims in order to avoid any bloodshed).

But the true absurdity of Charles Manson's claim that Linda was the ring-leader for the murders could be seen in the fact that she'd only been with the Family for about two months. Certainly no one who knew anything about the Family would have thought for a second she would have been able to usurp power over the Family from Manson. But the jury didn't know the Family. Would they believe it?

The rest of the copy cat motive would be left as close to the truth as possible so there would be sufficient corroborating evidence.

The final (fictional) version would run something like this; Linda Kasabian was madly in love with Bobby Beausoleil. When Beausoleil was arrested she became frantic to find a way to free him. She then came up with the idea of performing copy cat murders so the police would see the murders were continuing and conclude they must have arrested the wrong man. Beausoleil would be freed and the Family would be back together and she would be with Beausoleil again. She had convinced the other girls in the Family and together they had lured the men in to help them. And all without breathing a word to Manson.

Immediately Manson began dictating this version of the story to the members of the Family who weren't arrested, namely Lynette Fromme, Sandra Good, and Catherine Share. He would then have his lawyers call these people as witnesses during the penalty phase of the trial to try to sell the story to the jury.

And this is what he did. The problem was that most of these girls weren't closely related to the group who had gone out on the nights of August 8th and 9th. That whole group was now in jail. So it was easy for the prosecution to shed doubt not only on their testimony but on their motives and credibility as well. To make things worse, many of the girls called to testify didn't have the story down straight and others over-acted. This just gave the jury the impression Charles Manson was orchestrating a cover up – which is exactly what he was doing.[205]

Worse still for Charles Manson it showed the jury, once again, the depth of his manipulation and control over the people in his Family. It became more than obvious he *did* have the power to order people murdered and no one in the Family would have done anything he hadn't told them to do. No one would have taken control away from him, not Watson and certainly not a twenty-one year old Linda Kasabian.

The odd thing about all of this is that the prosecution knew this version of the copy-cat motive wasn't true. But by now they also knew about the connection between Gary Hinman's death and the Cielo/LaBianca killings, and they even knew about the incident with Bernard Crowe. So they knew the Helter Skelter motive was at least somewhat, if not completely, wrong.

But they'd gone to the moon and back to sell the Helter Skelter theory, and the jury had believed it. The prosecution couldn't possibly admit that perhaps Helter Skelter *wasn't* the motive. They would have lost all credibility.

---

[205] "In a conversation with her in early April of 1994, she [Catherine Share] acknowledged to me what I had already known... that her testimony was untruthful. She said ...that she had testified to it under his [Manson's] explicit direction." (*Helter Skelter*, AFTERWORD, pg. 511)

And this could all be traced back to the public pressure the District Attorney's Office had been under which forced them to rush the case to the Grand Jury before they fully understood everything that had happened. This book, of course, is meant to address this mistake. But in the case of the prosecution it meant they were locked into the Helter Skelter theory from that moment on.

They were stuck with Helter Skelter.

The Myth of Helter Skelter

Chapter 26

Suicide on Command

When it became obvious the poorly rehearsed and disjointed testimony of these girls wasn't going to be enough to get Charles Manson off the hook, he did something that showed his character much more clearly than anything other than the murder of Gary Hinman, the man who'd helped feed his son.

When Lynette Fromme, Sandra Good and Catherine Share perjured themselves on the stand for Charles Manson during the penalty phase of the trial they did so with little or nothing to lose. But when he came to Patricia Krenwinkel, Leslie Van Houten and myself and told us we were going have to get on the stand and claim we had deliberately and remorselessly, and with no direction from him at all, committed all the murders ourselves, he was basically telling us to commit suicide.[206]

---

[206] "[Manson] ... re-emphasized it, adding, "I'm a very selfish guy. I don't give a fuck for these girls. I'm only out for myself.""
(*Helter Skelter*, pg. 545)

That this request came so easy for him was probably the nastiest point in my life at that time. That he was brutal and cruel at times I already knew. That he was capable of murder, even the murder of a friend, I had known since watching him take a swing at Gary Hinman's head with a machete. That it appeared I was being set up for the murders ever since recanting my Grand Jury testimony was a thought I had tried to keep from my mind. But I had always assured myself, though cruelty and brutality seemed to surface in Manson at times, it was only because of the dire straits we had been in at Spahn Ranch. I had assured myself that all those words Manson had said about one big Family where everyone cared about everyone else and was willing to make sacrifices for one another were true.

That day I had to stop pretending and face the fact that all those sentiments were nothing but words to Charles Manson. The two and a half years I had spent with his Family overcoming adversity, struggling to get along, struggling to make ends meet, partying, hoping for the future, enjoying his dreams of being a musician, and scrimping though the hard times meant absolutely nothing to Charles Manson. *I* meant nothing to Charles Manson. None of the young people who'd come to follow and look up to Charles Manson meant anything to him, they were all expendable.[207] That was the day I really began to understand Charles Manson the way I do today — the way I'm showing him in this book.

By this time in the trial I no longer even had my conscientious attorney Richard Caballero to turn to. I had replaced him, at Manson's order, with one of Charles Manson's attorneys — Daye Shinn. Both of my codefendants had replaced their lawyers with one of Charles Manson's lawyers as well (Patricia Krenwinkel's attorney had simply been converted).[208, 209, 210] At this point in the trial, and faced with Manson's request, there was nowhere at all to turn.

---

[207] "[Bugliosi asks Manson]... why would they do what they're doing for you? Why would they be willing to follow you anywhere -- even to the gas chamber at San Quentin?" "Because I tell them the truth," Manson replied. "Other guys bullshit them and say 'I love you and only you' and all that baloney. I'm honest with them. I tell them I'm the most selfish guy in the world. And I am." (*Helter Skelter*, pg. 545)

[208] "Only later would we learn what was happening behind the scenes. Manson had set up his own communications network. Whenever he heard that an attorney for one of the girls had initiated a move on behalf of his client which could conceivably run counter to Manson's own defense, within days that attorney would be removed from the case." (*Helter Skelter*, pg. 269)

[209] "...attorney Marvin Part requested that a court-appointed psychiatrist examine his client, Leslie Van Houten. ...Though the prosecution would neither hear the tape not see the report, it was a fairly safe assumption that Part, like his predecessor Barnett, was considering an insanity plea. We didn't have to wait very long for Manson's reaction. On the nineteenth Leslie

The Myth of Helter Skelter

Throughout the whole trial I had been hoping Manson and the lawyers had some idea what they were doing. Charles Manson always said everything was going to work out all right. I didn't realize what he meant was everything was going to work out all right for him because, if worse came to worse, he had a back-up plan. That his plan was simply to sacrifice my codefendants and me was an idea I had refused to accept up to that point.[211, 212, 213]

---

requested that Part be relieved as her attorney and Ira Reiner appointed instead." (*Helter Skelter*, pg. 288)

[210] "Ira Reiner had been fired for one reason, and one reason only. He had tried to represent his client to the best of his ability. And he had properly decided that his client was not Charles Manson but Leslie Van Houten. There was a slight but perceptible smile on Manson's face. With good reason. He had succeeded in forming a unified defense team. Although Fitzgerald remained its nominal head, it was obvious who was calling the shots." (*Helter Skelter*, pg. 418)

[211] "...In discussing the many criminal activities of the Family, Manson had told Springer: "No matter what happens, the girls will take the rap for it."" (*Helter Skelter*, pg. 338)

[212] "By now it should be obvious to me [Bugliosi], Manson said, that the girls were acting on their own, that nobody was dominating them." (*Helter Skelter*, pg. 486)

[213] "Sadie [Atkins], Katie [Krenwinkel], and Leslie [Van Houten] wanted to take the stand and testify that they had planned and committed the murders -- and that Manson was not involved! ...On returning to open court, Kanarek made the motion to sever Manson so he could be tried separately. Charlie was now attempting to abandon ship, while letting the girls sink. After denying the motion, [Judge] Older had the jury brought

Suicide on Command

We should have refused.

But Charles Manson was an expert manipulator. He'd waited to the end to tell us this was his back-up plan on purpose. By this time in the trial, he said, there was only one hope for all of us and that was to discredit the prosecution's case. We couldn't defend ourselves from all his charges, Manson said, but we could throw dirt on Linda Kasabian and completely undermine the Helter Skelter motive. If we could convince the jury the prosecution was completely wrong about the motive for the murders there was a chance they could be persuaded they hadn't been

---

in... Shinn [Defense Attorney for Atkins] said he would ask to be relieved as counsel if Older ordered him to question his client. Fitzgerald replied similarly, adding, "As far as I am concerned, it would be sort of aiding and abetting a suicide." ...The following day Manson surprised everyone by saying that he too wanted to testify... ...he requested and received permission to make a statement [outside the presence of the jury]. He spoke for over an hour... [Trial testimony:] "If I showed them that I would do anything for my brother -- including giving my life for my brother on the battlefield-- and they pick up their banner, and they go off and do what they do, that is not my responsibility. I don't tell people what to do..." "These children [indicating the female defendants] were finding themselves. What they did, if they did whatever they did, is up to them. They will have to explain that to you..." ... "I have killed no one and I have ordered no one to be killed.'" (*Helter Skelter*, pg. 523 - 527)

given the whole story. They may come to believe there might be mitigating circumstances the prosecution hid.

This tactic didn't work. All four of us ended up on death row. But Manson should have known it wouldn't work. He made the same mistake he had with the testimony from the other girls in the Family — our stories were thrown together and poorly rehearsed, they were obviously concocted for the sole purpose of slandering Linda Kasabian and removing Charles Manson from the crimes, and they were only more proof to the jury that Charles Manson was in complete control of the Family, even unto death.[214, 215] Charles Manson had been beat — or rather, he'd beat himself.

Once again, it illustrates the self-interested purpose of Charles Manson to point out that during the penalty phase of the Cielo/LaBianca trial, he not

---

[214] [Bugliosi's opening statements for penalty phase] "When Atkins, Krenwinkel, and Van Houten played the part of the sacrificial lamb and admitted their participation in these murders, and then lied on that witness stand and said that Manson wasn't involved, the fact that they were willing to lie on that witness stand just proves, all the more, Manson's domination over them....'" (*Helter Skelter*, pg. 609)

[215] "Next, under California law, came a so-called penalty trial ...It was a chaotic, dragged-out affair in which we did all we could to throw everything into confusion by changing our stories all around and trying to prove Charlie innocent." (*Child of Satan, Child of God*, pg. 167 & 168)

only instructed us to confess to those murders but he made us confess to the murder of Gary Hinman. This was a completely uncorroborated story and it was ridiculous for many reasons, the most obvious being that neither Patricia Krenwinkel or Leslie Van Houten had even been to Gary Hinman's home.[216]

What's more, Mary Brunner had already testified it was Bobby Beausoleil who had killed Gary Hinman. And Bobby Beausoleil, in an attempt to extricate himself, had claimed Manson had killed Gary. Both accounts made it very unlikely my co-defendants or I could have done it. After all, if Beausoleil was trying to save his skin it would have been a lot easier to claim I had killed Gary than to have claimed anyone else had, and it would have been the first thing on his mind if I actually *had* killed Gary.

But what makes this maneuver interesting is that Manson was already trying to expedite himself from being convicted for the murder of Gary Hinman even before he'd been charged with Gary's death. He was already trying to set up a defense.

His first plan had been simply to distance himself physically from the murders. Now it was obvious the ridiculous Helter Skelter motive could be

---

[216] "In discussing the Hinman murder, Susan had placed Leslie Van Houten at the murder scene. There had never been any evidence whatsoever that Leslie was involved in the Hinman murder." (*Helter Skelter*, pg. 577)

used to convict him even though he wasn't at the crime scene when the murders took place. But that had been his whole master plan. He'd gone to a lot of trouble to distance himself physically from the murders and now it wouldn't help him at all.

So now my codefendants and I had to swear we killed Gary Hinman without Manson's encouragement. In fact, now the death of Gary Hinman was changed to look more like self defense. But the whole story was now so ridiculous nobody believed it.

Even subtler is the fact that Charles Manson was trying to get us to admit to the murder of Gary *without Bobby being involved*. The reason for this can be understood only if one tries to think what Manson would gain by this. He now knew he would be tried for Gary Hinman's death, and he knew he could be convicted if it could be shown that he had instigated the killing.

He knew his three codefendants could be forced to confess he had no part in the killing, but what about Bobby Beausoleil? Beausoleil had already let Manson know if he was convicted he'd implicate Manson, and now he was convicted. Bobby Beausoleil had also already testified, unconvincingly, at his second trial that Manson had done the killing. It was obvious Charles Manson was trying to throw Bobby Beausoleil a bone. If Charles Manson could force us to take the heat for Bobby Beausoleil, he might be able to convince Bobby not to testify against him. Manson might still be able to worm his way out of that charge.

Once again this ploy didn't work. And once again this was due mostly to poor story telling by myself and my codefendants. But what is of interest is the depth of Manson's manipulations.

Another example of Charles Manson's cold calculations was his attempt, in the later stages of the trial, to force Catherine Share to tell everyone she was carrying his child.[217] Her child was *not* Manson's son, and he knew it. He was simply trying to play on the hearts of the public and the jury members right before they were to decide whether to sentence him to death.

In the end my testimony and the testimony of my co-defendants was a joke. Our lawyers, learning that we intended to implicate ourselves, refused to question us. When we finally were allowed to give statements none of the stories worked together. They contradicted each other. They didn't make sense.

But by this time I really didn't care. I was testifying simply to protect myself and to get Manson off my back. I didn't care if the stories didn't make sense. I didn't care if they weren't convincing. And I honestly didn't care if the jury believed them. I was

---

[217] Share: "It was a pretty hard experience. Charlie wanted me to tell them that he was the father. And I was programmed... I mean, I--we were sent notes constantly, "do this, do that, do the other thing." (Channel 2, Cover Story, 1993, KCBS, reporter: Harvey Levin)

already convicted and looking at the death penalty — why should Manson walk away free?[218]

This is also when I was told to say I killed Sharon Tate.

The reason Manson told me to claim it was me who killed Sharon Tate should be obvious. Just like when Manson made us "confess" to killing Gary Hinman without Beausoleil in order to buy Bobby's silence if Manson was charged with Gary's death, Manson was making us "confess" to killing everyone at the Cielo Dr. and LaBianca homes without Charles Watson. If Manson could get us to take responsibility for those crimes without Watson being involved, then that would give Watson a defense when he finally faced trial.

Manson was still planning on appealing his case and what he didn't want to happen was to successfully appeal his conviction and then have the DA's make a deal with Watson in exchange for Watson testifying against Manson.

And so I said I killed Sharon Tate. By that time it hardly seemed important — I was numb after months and months of pressure from both the District Attorneys and Manson's minions. While my two co-

---

[218] "On questioning, the defendant [Susan] stated that she did not think she would end up in the gas chamber, but "if I do, it's alright." ..." (Susan's Probation Officer's Report, 4-19-71)

defendants at least had each other to confide in, I had no one. Though we stood together in the pictures for the newspapers, no one would even talk to me. They blamed me for getting everyone indicted.

This was another reason I went along with Manson's plan and "confessed" to killing Sharon Tate. Besides the constant threats and pressure from Manson, I realized I'd already been convicted. What ever the outcome, either life in prison or the death penalty, I was going to prison and I was going to be locked up with these two women. My best hope was to mend that rift and try to get "back in the fold."

My testimony during the Penalty Phase of the trial was so ridiculous the Prosecutor claimed the holes in my story were a mile wide.[219] In fact he used my Grand Jury testimony as proof I was lying.[220]

Unfortunately for me if you lie under oath, or if you tell two different stories under oath, the prosecution can use your inconsistencies to discredit the parts of your story they don't want to accept, while

---

[219] "The holes in her story were a mile wide. I noted them for my cross-examination." (*Helter Skelter*, pg. 576)

[220] "Since Susan had now testified to these matters, the prosecution was able to use her prior inconsistent statements – including her grand jury testimony – for impeachment purposes." (*Helter Skelter*, pg. 579-580) [Editor's Note: Impeachment is when you use a witness's prior statements under oath to discredit their present testimony.]

the parts of your story they want to use they can call a "confession."[221]

Though the Prosecutor admits that almost everything I said during my Penalty Phase testimony was a lie, he can still claim I "confessed" under oath I killed Sharon Tate. And there's nothing I can do about it.[222]

Unfortunately in our Legal System, if you choose to commit suicide on the stand there's nothing anyone can do to stop you.

---

[221] Here is an example from Helter Skelter, regarding the question of how Susan could have stabbed Voytek Frykowski and Sharon Tate as the prosecution insisted when there was no blood on her knife: "Why was there no blood on the Buck knife [Susan's knife] found in the chair? ... We had no answer. We could speculate, however, that Sadie lost her knife before she stabbed Voytek and Sharon, possibly while she was in the process of tying up Voytek, and that at some later point she borrowed another knife from Katie or Tex. Much more important than what knife she used was the fact that she *confessed* stabbing both of the victims to Virginia Graham and Ronnie Howard." (*Helter Skelter*, pg. 548, emphasis added.)

[222] "Although by this time all counsel knew that the three girls intended to take the stand and "confess," Fitzgerald having mentioned it in chambers nearly a week before..." [quotation marks in original] (*Helter Skelter*, pg. 575)

Suicide on Command

The Myth of Helter Skelter

Chapter 27

The Difference Between Vampires and Angels

There are a lot of reasons to believe I did not kill Sharon Tate.

I won't waste your time asking you to take my word for it. This book is absolutely worthless if the reader isn't skeptical. I'll simply lay down what other people have said and you can weigh it as you see fit.

I've already shown my exaggeration of my part in the crime when I was talking to Virginia Graham and Ronnie Howard in County Jail was in line with Manson's own admission that this is exactly what he'd told us to do if we were ever arrested. It is also in line with Graham and Howard's own assessments that I was simply exaggerating in order to look tough and hide the fact I was scared.

And I've shown that even the Prosecutor admits my testimony on the witness stand during the penalty phase of the trial was almost complete nonsense directed by Manson with the sole purpose of shifting the responsibility for the crimes off Manson and onto myself and my co-defendants.

And I've shown if my present claim that I didn't kill Sharon Tate is a lie then it's one I made up over thirty years ago and have stuck to ever since.

I can also point to the fact that I said I hadn't killed Sharon Tate during my Grand Jury testimony in 1969. This was the testimony I was told by the Prosecutor had to be true or I could be executed. That's a strong incentive to tell the truth.

Mr. Bugliosi, of course, believes I lied about that part of the crime in my Grand Jury testimony. I am happy to point out that even Mr. Bugliosi admits my rendition of the crimes as told to the Grand Jury was corroborated in every instance by the version Linda Kasabian gave.[223, 224, 225] And what makes this

---

[223] "Though she added many details, Linda Kasabian's story of those two nights was basically the same as Susan Atkins'." (*Helter Skelter*, pg. 344)

[224] "Just the discovery of the wallet was enough for me, for it provided another piece of independent evidence supporting Susan Atkins' story." [statement of Vincent Bugliosi] (*Helter Skelter*, pg. 256)

[225] "Eventually he [Manson] told her [Kasabian] to stop in front of a house, which Linda described as a modern one-story, middle-class-type home. This was the place where, as described by Susan Atkins, Manson got out, had them drive around the block, then got back in, telling them that, having looked in the window and seen photographs of children, he didn't want to

all the more impressive is that Linda never heard my Grand Jury testimony, nor could she in any way be induced to conform her story to mine — there was no reason to, she'd already been given complete immunity.

Though Linda was not present in the Cielo House when Sharon Tate was killed, and therefore can not confirm or deny that part of my story, it carries a certain weight that in every instance where our stories can be compared they corroborate one another.

While none of this is proof in itself, it does indicate there is a real possibility what I say is true. But even beyond this there are numerous objective indications my story is true.

I've already mentioned Charles Watson has stated I didn't kill Sharon Tate.[226, 227, 228]

"do" that particular house... Linda's account was essentially the same as Susan's." (*Helter Skelter*, pg. 362)

[226] [Chaplain Ray recalling his 1975 conversation with Charles Watson, "I then remembered one of the reasons for my visit. "The last thing Susan Atkins said to me," I told Tex, "was that her hands had never taken a human life. You were there when the people at the Tate mansion were killed. You were there when the LaBiancas were murdered. Only you can tell me if Susan is telling the truth." "She's telling the truth," Tex Watson said. "She didn't kill anyone." (*God's Prison Gang*, Paperback version, pg. 35)

[227] "Later, Prosecutor Bugliosi - because of some things Susan-Sadie bragged about in jail in one of her attempts to get

The Myth of Helter Skelter

In addition, the Prosecutor has since admitted the knife I was carrying the night Sharon Tate was killed was actually found at the crime scene. It was tested for blood and it was found to be clean.[229] It had never struck anyone.

This evidence about the knife is strange for several reasons. The primary reason is because I didn't know about this until sometime around 1990 when I worked with several lawyers who, at their own expense and on their own time, actually went back and checked the prosecutor's account of the crime. I honestly don't remember anything about this at the trial.

---

attention - was convinced that it was she who killed Sharon Tate, but his suspicion was not true." (*Will You Die For Me?*, paperback version pg. 137, hardback version, pg; 143)

[228] "She [Susan] exaggerated other things, however, such as claiming that she had stabbed Sharon... ... Later, Susan-Sadie herself told her story to the D.A.'s office and then to the grand jury (a more factual version that left out her claim to having stabbed Sharon Tate)..." (*Will You Die For Me?*, hardback version, pg; 161)

[229] "[Officer] Granado found the second knife in the living room, less than three feet from Sharon Tate's body. It was wedged behind the cushion in one of the chairs, with the blade sticking up. A buck brand clasp-type pocketknife, its blade was ¾ inch in diameter, 3 13/16 inches in length, making it too small to have caused most of the wounds. Noticing a spot on the side of the blade, Granado tested it for blood: negative." (*Helter Skelter*, pg. 23)

The Difference Between Vampires and Angels

There is no dispute it was my knife, as Linda Kasabian was the one who handed out the knives and she identified it. And there is no dispute there was no blood on it. But I have been told the Prosecutor has none the less insisted the fact my knife wasn't used doesn't prove I didn't kill Sharon Tate at all, claiming I could have borrowed Charles Watson's knife.[230]

The only problem with this explanation is if I'd had to ask Charles Watson for *his* knife he would have discovered I'd lost *my* knife while we were still in the house. But Linda Kasabian testified Watson didn't discover this until after the crimes when Linda was collecting the weapons and I had to admit I'd lost my knife in the house. According to Linda Kasabian, Watson became very upset and yelled at me.[231] We then discussed whether we should go back and look

---

[230] "Why was there no blood on the Buck knife found in the chair? Kanarek had raised this point. It was a good one. We had no answer. We could speculate, however, that Sadie [Susan] lost her knife before she stabbed Voytek and Sharon, possibly while she was in the process of tying up Voytek, and that at some later point she borrowed another knife from Katie [Patricia Krenwinkel] or Tex [Charles Watson]." (*Helter Skelter*, pg. 548)

[231] "Tex yelled at me [Linda Kasabian] to turn off the car and get over." ... Linda slid over to the passenger side. "Then he started in on Sadie [Susan] and yelled at her for losing her knife."" (*Helter Skelter*, pg. 354)

for it.[232] In the end none of us wanted to go back in the house.

Whether you find this compelling or not, it is the prosecution itself that put forward the proof Watson didn't discover I'd lost my knife until after the crime. It's hard to insist Watson could have loaned me his knife without noticing my hands were already empty.[233]

Linda Kasabian, who was standing guard at the end of the front walkway, also testified that when the crimes began she at first ran to the front door to find me and implore me to make the others stop. It was her

---

[232] "After they'd left the Tate residence, Susan continued, she discovered that she had lost her knife. ... They had thought about going back to look for it but had decided against it." (*Helter Skelter*, pg. 115)

[233] [Editor's Note: In Susan's 1977 autobiography she actually says she remembers getting a second knife from Linda Kasabian. "Just then Linda came back in. "Give me your knife," I yelled. "I've lost mine." Apparently Linda did give me her knife, for I soon had another one. My own turned out to have fallen between cushions on the couch and was to be found by police the next day." (*Child of Satan, Child of God*, pg. 141) But this contradicts all the other evidence in the case, including Linda Kasabian's testimony that there were only three knives and that she'd already given her own knife to Patricia Krenwinkel and therefore didn't have a knife to hand to Susan. When I showed Susan the trial evidence she simply said the story she related in 1977 was what she thought had happened.]

The Difference Between Vampires and Angels

testimony that I held out my hands and said I couldn't.[234]

Either way, whether you believe me or not is only an intellectual point — conspiracy to commit a crime makes you morally and legally culpable whether you struck the actual blow or not. I was convicted for those deaths and whether I physically partook of the crime or not doesn't matter legally.

The reason it becomes interesting at all is because it has a very strong bearing on the difference between a Vampire and an Angel.

During his final summation, right before the jury was sent out to determine whether to put me to death, the Prosecutor told them I was a blood-drinking vampire.[235] In contrast he has claimed that Linda Kasabian was an Angel — a "true flower child." [236]

---

[234] "Linda Kasabian's account: "And then [right after Frykowski fell into the bushes] Sadie [Susan] came running out of the house, and I said, 'Sadie, please make it stop! People are coming!' Which wasn't true, but I wanted to make it stop. And she said, 'It's too late.'" Complaining that she had lost her knife, Susan ran back into the house. Linda remained outside. (Susan had earlier told me, and the grand jury, that Linda had never entered the residence.)" (*Helter Skelter*, pg. 354)
[235] "Susan Atkins, the vampira, actually tasted Sharon Tate's blood..." (*Helter Skelter*, pg. 553)
[236] From the movie *Manson*, narrated by Vincent Bugliosi.

I believe the truth is Mr. Bugliosi realizes there are a lot of reasons to believe I did not actually kill Sharon Tate, but I also believe it will be almost impossible for him to ever admit that. The reason is because if he admits I probably didn't kill Sharon Tate he has to deal with the fact that I was nearly executed. This should bother him because if I didn't kill Sharon Tate then there is absolutely no level upon which Linda Kasabian was less culpable than I was.

Linda had been with the Family for less than two months when she participated in the deaths of seven human beings.[237, 238] Manson had over two years to threaten and pressure me.

Linda had two parents, separated, and an ex-husband she could have escaped to (and eventually did). I had no one in the world to turn to.[239]

Linda claimed she participated because of fears for her two-year-old daughter. I had a ten-month-old, two-month premature son to fear for.

Linda had sharpened the knives at Spahn Ranch, I hadn't.[240]

---

[237] "But she [Kasabian] didn't stay long [DeCarlo told LA Sheriffs], maybe only a month or so and he didn't know much about her." (*Helter Skelter*, pg. 149)

[238] "She [Kasabian] had remained with the Family less than a month and a half..." (*Helter Skelter*, pg. 343)

[239] "For Susan, I realized, the Family was her only family." [Vincent Bugliosi] (*Helter Skelter*, pg. 255)

The Difference Between Vampires and Angels

Linda had carried a knife that night, just as I had.[241]

Linda had driven the car on both crime nights. I had not.

Linda stood watch outside the Cielo Dr. residence. I had not.

Linda ran away from the crime scene at Cielo Dr.. I had frozen and had not been able to participate.

Linda collected the weapons and clothing after the Cielo Dr. crime. I had not.

Linda discarded the weapons and clothing after the Cielo Dr. crime. I had not.[242]

After the Cielo Dr. crime, when Manson asked all of us if we had any remorse Linda claimed she did not – just as I had.[243]

---

[240] "Linda – who, on Manson's instructions, had several times honed knives similar to these while at Spahn Ranch – testified that the knives were sharpened on both sides, on one side all the way back to the hilt, on the other at least an inch back from the tip." (*Helter Skelter*, pg. 457)

[241] "Linda couldn't find her own knife (Sadie had it), but she obtained one from Larry Jones. The handle was broken and had been replaced with tape." (*Helter Skelter*, pg. 350)

[242] "He [Watson] stopped the car on a dirt shoulder off the road, and Tex, Sadie, and Katie gave Linda their bloody clothing, which, on Tex's instructions, she rolled up in one bundle and threw down the slope." (*Helter Skelter*, pg. 355)

[243] "Manson asked the four, "Do you have any remorse?" All shook their heads and said "No." Linda did feel remorse, she told me, but she didn't admit it to Charlie because "I was afraid

The Myth of Helter Skelter

Linda had gone out the next night fearing what would happen, just as I had.[244]

Linda had driven Manson to the LaBianca home, I hadn't.[245]

Linda stayed in the car at the LaBianca crime scene, just as I had.[246]

Linda accepted Ms. LaBianca's stolen wallet from Manson. I hadn't.[247]

Linda had deposited Ms. LaBianca's wallet at a gas station so the police would suspect a black person. I hadn't.[248]

---

for my life. I could see in his eyes he knew how I felt. And it was against his way.'"" (*Helter Skelter*, pg. 356)

[244] ""I just looked at him and, you know, just sort of pleaded with my eyes, please don't make me go, because," Linda said, "I just knew we were going out again, and I knew it would be the same thing, but I was afraid to say anything.'"" (*Helter Skelter*, pg. 361)

[245] "Manson told Linda to take over the driving. ... Following Manson's directions, Linda took the freeway to Pasadena." (*Helter Skelter*, pg. 362)

[246] "Susan Atkins herself hadn't been inside the LaBianca residence. She had remained in the car with Clem and Linda." (*Helter Skelter*, pg. 226)

[247] "As the trio started towards the house, Manson got back into the car and handed Linda a woman's wallet, telling her to wipe off the prints and remove the change. In opening it she noticed the driver's license, which had a photo of a woman with dark hair." (*Helter Skelter*, pg. 364)

[248] "Manson told Linda that when they reached a predominantly colored area he wanted her to toss the wallet out

The Difference Between Vampires and Angels

Linda stopped the car so Manson could attempt to kill another motorist. I hadn't.[249]

Linda told Manson where another victim might be found the night of the LaBianca crime. I had not.[250]

Linda showed Manson where the other potential victim lived. I had not.[251]

Linda didn't go to the police even after she'd escaped from Spahn Ranch while I agreed to help the police even when I was in jail and was being threatened for being a "snitch."

---

onto a sidewalk, so a black person would find it, use the credit cards, and be arrested." (*Helter Skelter*, pg. 365)

[249] "Observing a white sports car ahead of them, Manson told Linda, "At the next red light, pull up beside it. I'm going to kill the driver." Linda pulled up next to the car, but just as Manson jumped out, the light changed to green and the sports car zoomed away." (*Helter Skelter*, pg. 362-363)

[250] "Manson told Linda to drive to Venice [after the beach]. En route he asked the three if they knew anyone there. None did. Manson then asked Linda, "What about the man you and Sandy met in Venice? Wasn't he a piggy?" Linda replied, "Yes, he's an actor." Manson told her to drive to his apartment." (*Helter Skelter*, pg. 366)

[251] "However, she [Kasabian] felt sure she could find the apartment house, as she had located it when Manson asked her to drive there that night. When they pulled up in front, Manson asked Linda it the man could let her in. "I think so," she replied. What about Sadie and Clem? Linda said she guessed so. Manson then handed her a pocketknife and demonstrated how he wanted her to slit the actor's throat." (*Helter Skelter*, pg. 366)

Linda didn't go to the police even after she got her daughter back. I agreed to testify even though I never got my son back.[252]

Linda didn't go to the police even when she and her daughter moved all the way to New York.

Linda only offered to make a deal with the District Attorney's Office after she'd been indicted. I had agreed to work with the police as soon as I was implicated.

Linda only agreed to testified against Manson on condition she be given absolute immunity for her part in the deaths of seven people. I had agreed to testify against Manson and still go to trial for my part in the crime.[253]

Linda hadn't been the one to break the case to the police. I was.

Linda hadn't been the one who got Charles Manson indicted. I was.

---

[252] "I asked Linda, "Why, between the time you reclaimed Tanya and the date of your arrest in December, didn't you contact the police and tell them what you knew about the murders?" She was afraid of Mason, Linda said, afraid that he might find and kill both her and Tanya. Also, she was pregnant, and didn't want to go through this ordeal until after the baby was born." (*Helter Skelter*, pg. 391)

[253] "In accordance with the earlier discussion between our office and LAPD, we said that if Susan would cooperate with us, we would probably let her plead guilty to second degree murder – i.e. we would not seek the death sentence, but we would ask for life imprisonment." (*Helter Skelter*, pg. 214)

The Difference Between Vampires and Angels

Linda didn't go out with the police to try to find evidence. I did.²⁵⁴

Mr. Bugliosi claims Linda told him she still loved Manson even after watching him orchestrate the murder of seven people, even during the trial.²⁵⁶ I never claimed that.

The only point upon which my part in the crimes appears greater than Linda's is if one insists I killed Sharon Tate.

Once that assertion is questioned it becomes very hard to determine why I was the Vampire and Linda was the Angel... other than the fact the prosecutor had to explain to the public why he was letting Linda go scott free at the same time he was asking the jury to put me to death.²⁵⁵

It may be cynical but it has to be pointed out that Mr. Bugliosi's book about the crime was published just before he ran for Attorney General of

---

²⁵⁴ "To date LAPD hadn't even begun looking for the Tate weapons and clothing, although Susan Atkins' statement gave us some good clues as to the general area where they should be. Arrangements were made through out office for Susan to be taken from Sybil Brand the following Sunday, to see if she could point out the spots where Linda Kasabian had thrown the various items." (*Helter Skelter*, pg. 257)

²⁵⁵ "As noted, given a choice between Susan and Linda, I'd preferred Linda, sight unseen: she hadn't killed anyone and therefore would be far more acceptable to a jury than the bloodthirsty Susan." (*Helter Skelter*, pg. 342)

California. It wouldn't have looked good to have to admit Mr. Bugliosi had allowed Linda to walk away from seven counts of first degree murder simply because that was the deal he had to make. It was much better to insist she was given complete immunity because she wasn't culpable – she was an innocent "Angel." In fact, Mr. Bugliosi went so far as to claim he thought people would understandable how she could still love Charles Manson even after watching him orchestrate seven murders.[256]

I can't.

But Mr. Bugliosi also had to explain why, if I was so bad, the District Attorney's Office had agreed to make a deal with me. Mr. Bugliosi's account of the crime and trial is very detailed about his own insistence he'd always been against giving me any consideration.[257, 258, 259] Whether or not it was true it

---

[256] "...he [Manson] and Linda walked ahead in the sand [after the murder of Leno and Rosemary LaBianca]. ...Linda told Charlie that she was pregnant. Manson took Linda's hand and, as she described it, "it was sort of nice, you know, we were just talking, I gave him some peanuts, and he just sort of made me forget about everything, made me feel good." Would the jury understand this? I thought so, once they understood Manson's charismatic personality and Linda's love for him." (*Helter Skelter*, pg. 365-366)

[257] "LAPD wanted to offer Susan Atkins immunity, in exchange for telling what she knew about the murders. ...I was in total disagreement. "If what she told Ronnie Howard is true, Atkins personally stabbed to death Sharon Tate, Gary Hinman,

was a smart thing to say right before one runs for Attorney General.

But all this isn't an indictment of Linda. I know exactly the pressure she was under. And I know exactly what Linda was doing. She was doing what ever it took to stay alive and keep her daughter alive until she could figure out how to escape.[260] She was putting on an act so Manson — the man who'd killed his friend Gary Hinman when he insisted he didn't have any money and who'd had Donald Shea killed because he thought Shea had called the police on him

---

and who knows how many others! *We don't give that gal anything!*'" (*Helter Skelter*, pg. 164-5, emphasis in original.)
[258] "Let's see if, on our own, we can get enough evidence to nail all of them. If we can't then, as a last resort – a very, very last resort – we can turn to Atkins." (*Helter Skelter*, pg. 165)
[259] "[LAPD Lieutenant] LaPage was firm; LAPD wanted to make a deal. I conferred with Busch and Stovitz; they were far less adamant than I. Against my very strong objections, Busch told LePage that the DA's Office would be willing to settle for a second degree murder plea for Atkins." (*Helter Skelter*, pg. 165)
[260] "Linda turned and ran down the driveway [of the Cielo Dr. residence]. For what seemed like maybe five minutes, she hid in the bushes near the gate, then climbed the fence again and ran down Cielo to where they had parked the Ford. Q. "Why didn't you run to one of the houses and call the police?" I asked Linda. A. "My first thought was 'Get help!' Then my little girl entered my mind – she was back [at the ranch] with Charlie. I didn't know where I was or how to get out of there.'" (*Helter Skelter*, pg. 354)

— wouldn't suspect she was simply waiting for a moment to run.

I know this. I know it even better than the prosecuting attorney. I know it because I was there. My son was being held by armed guards right along with Linda's daughter.[261] I stood right beside her after the crimes as she told Manson she had no regrets out of fear, and I did the same.

And I understand why she ran to New York and hid and didn't tell the police even after she retrieved her daughter from Manson's grasp. She was afraid. I understand this because I was afraid of him too.[262]

Linda did what she had to do to survive. And when the time came she did what she should have and she testified against Manson. I've never held that

---

[261] "Linda told me that she decided to flee after the night of the LaBianca murders; however, Manson sent her to the waterfall area later that day [where the children had been moved] and she was afraid to leave that night because of the armed guards he had posted." (*Helter Skelter*, pg. 389)

[262] "Mr. Bugliosi:
Q Are you a little nervous?
A I'm scared to death.
Q Well, most people who do testify in court are a little frightened, Susan, so it is not unusual." (Grand Jury Transcripts, pg. 10)

The Difference Between Vampires and Angels

against her, even though by doing so she testified against me as well.[263]

But I had been faced with quite a different situation. I could have either testified against Manson and then spent my life in prison trying to avoid getting killed by his minions and hoping they never found my son (remember, my deal was simply that I wouldn't get the death penalty, I was still going to prison). Or I could have recanted my testimony and taken a chance we wouldn't be found guilty and I would have known no matter what the outcome of the trial my son would be safe.

Linda was faced with the choice of either testifying against Manson and walking away completely free, or refusing to testify and facing the death penalty.

Linda made the right choice and it's a choice I wish I'd had the opportunity to make, but I had been faced with a much different situation than she was.

[Editor's Note: In the subsequent Wrongful Death Lawsuit filed after the criminal trial, Linda Kasabian was found to be equally responsible with Manson, Watson, Krenwinkel, and Susan for the deaths of the five people at Cielo Drive, including

---

[263] "On questioning, the defendant [Susan] stated... She does not hold Linda [Kasabian's] position in the prosecution against her..." (Susan's Probation Officer's Report, 4-19-71)

Sharon Tate, and Linda Kasabian was held joint and severally liable for millions of dollars in damages.]

Chapter 28

Life and Death Concurrently

In the end we were all sentenced to death for the seven murders that occurred at the Cielo Dr. and LaBianca residences. Then we began the trial for Gary Hinman's death.

By this time I was exhausted emotionally and mentally by the trial and the continuing isolation my co-defendants were putting me through. As soon as the trial for Gary's death began I agreed to plead guilty. I did it to get out of that courtroom and away from Manson.

But when they asked me if I went to Gary's house as part of a robbery, I told them the truth — I didn't know Gary was going to be robbed.[264]

---

[264] "MR. KATZ [District Attorney]: And when you were at the home of Gary Alan Hinman, were you aware of and apprised of the fact that a robbery was taking place in connection with Gary Hinman's property?
***

Then they asked me if I knew we were going to Gary's house intending to kill him, and I told them the truth again — I didn't know Gary was going to die.[265]

At this point the Judge delicately pointed out to me that in order to plead guilty I had to actually confess to doing something wrong. Since I was being tried for first degree murder I had to admit to some form of premeditation or he couldn't accept my guilty plea. So I told him I killed Gary by suffocating him with a pillow.[266]

---

[265] "DEFENDANT ATKINS: ...I cannot honestly look at this court and say, "Yes, I was aware there was a robbery," because no, I was not aware the robbery was going on." (6-4-71, Plea Transcript, pgs. 7-8)

"MR. KATZ: ...were you aware, during that period of time, that there was an intention by others that were in your presence to kill Gary Alan Hinman?

DEFENDANT ATKINS: No." (6-4-71, Plea Transcript, pg. 8)

[266] "THE COURT: As a matter of fact, did you use a pillow in order to muffle his -- of, to cut off his breath?

DEFENDANT ATKINS: Your Honor, I don't understand this cross examination.

THE COURT: Well, the Court has to determine whether of not there's a factual basis. I won't accept this plea of guilty unless I know that you are in fact guilty; do you understand that?

DEFENDANT ATKINS: Yes. I wouldn't be making this plea, your Honor, unless in fact I knew I was guilty. Do you understand that?
***

Life and Death Concurrently

It was an odd thing to say. It wasn't true. But I just honestly didn't see any reason for sitting in that courtroom next to Manson for one more minute when I already had the death penalty.

The District Attorney got up and told the judge their evidence showed Gary had not been suffocated and they had never believed I'd killed him, but that they would accept my guilty plea because they believed I had known he was going to be robbed or killed and had gone there for that reason.[267]

The judge accepted my plea and sentenced me to life. I asked him whether I was supposed to serve that before or after my death penalty. I was told I would be serving them concurrently.

As for Manson, he was tried and convicted for the murder of Gary Hinman and received an additional death sentence.

THE COURT: All right. Well, let's get to the point now. Did you in fact do that which I am talking about -- with the pillow?

DEFENDANT ATKINS: Yes." (6-4-71, Plea Transcript, pg. 12)

[267] "MR KATZ: ...based upon the evidence which is presently available to the People, we believe that the evidence would show that Miss Atkins did not wield the death weapon, but rather is guilty of first degree murder on an aiding and abetting theory, and on a conspiracy theory to commit murder and robbery of Gary Alan Hinman." (6-4-71, Plea Transcript, pg. 13)

Bruce Davis was also convicted for Gary's death, though as far as I remember he merely showed up with Manson the afternoon Manson attacked Gary. He joined Bobby Beausoleil on death row.

A later trial for the death of Donald Shea was conducted, but since I had nothing to do with that I don't know the details. Manson was convicted again, as was Steve Grogan. The jury recommended the death penalty but the Judge gave Grogan life instead, claiming he had diminished capacity I believe.

Steve Grogan was paroled in 1985 after agreeing to lead authorities to the body of Donald Shea.[268] To their surprise, contrary to Grogan's boasting in 1969, Donald Shea's body hadn't been cut into pieces. That was just a story to try to scare Family members from talking to police.[269]

---

[268] "On November 18, 1985, Grogan was released from prison, and was discharged from parole on April 13, 1988." (*Helter Skelter*, AFTERWORD, pg. 509)

[269] "One of the enduring Manson Family mysteries was cleared up by Grogan. It had become part of Manson Family lore, possibly to frighten all members who had mutinous thought, that Shea was decapitated by Grogan and had been cut up and buried in nine separate places at Spahn Ranch. ... Subsequently, Sergeant Gleason and his partner found Shea's remains in one piece at the spot designated by Grogan – the bottom of a steep embankment about a quarter mile down the road from the ranch." (*Helter Skelter*, AFTERWORD, pg. 509)

Charles Watson was later tried for the Cielo Dr. and LaBianca crimes and was convicted as well. Though I don't know the details of that trial, I think because he was not under the threat of Manson he was able to put forward a much more realistic defense, at least acknowledging the incredible pressure everyone in the Family was under from Manson.

Late in 1971, Manson ordered Catherine Share and Mary Brunner to break another man out of jail. After the jailbreak the three of them, along with other members of the Family, instigated the robbery of a Hawthorne sporting goods store. Their goal was money and guns with which to break Charles Manson out of jail. They failed and another long line of people headed to prison, mislead by Charles Manson's talk of "brotherly love" and "self-sacrifice" — two concepts of which Charles Manson himself has no understanding of or use for at all.

The Myth of Helter Skelter

Chapter 29

Life After Death

After my conviction I was informed an appeal was being filed. It was being prepared by Charles Manson's attorneys. I wasn't informed as to what the issues were and no one came and talked to me about it. But having seen how Manson's attorneys worked during the trial I didn't hold out much hope.

And in 1976 the appeal was denied, with the exception of overturning Leslie Van Houten's conviction.

It wasn't until the 1990's that one of my attorneys actually looked up the appeal and read the Court's decision.

The opinion is a hundred and eight pages long, and buried deep down on page fifty-seven and fifty-eight are three small paragraphs under the heading of "Use of Perjured Testimony."

```
"Susan Atkins testified at the
grand jury proceedings but not
```

at trial; Roni Howard and Virginia Graham did not testify before the grand jury but did testify at trial. Manson draws attention to the fact that before the grand jury Atkins stated that Watson had killed Sharon Tate. At trial Graham and Howard testified that Atkins claimed she had killed Sharon Tate. From this conflict Manson argues... that he was convicted by the knowing use of perjured testimony

***

Manson makes much of BUGLIOSI'S testimony during the penalty phase to the effect that he believed Atkins did stab Tate even though he knew she would testify to the contrary before the grand jury. BUGLIOSI'S opinion on the subject is just that. The record does not reflect that the testimony was in fact perjured." (People v. Manson et al. (1976) 61 CAL.APP.3D 102)

So there it was. Almost a third of a century ago the California Courts determined my Grand Jury testimony was not perjured, explicitly concerning the

Life After Death

death of Sharon Tate. I hadn't killed Sharon Tate and the Court had held there was nothing in the record to indicate I was lying when I said I hadn't. And no one had ever told me.

In a related note, in 2009 I received a letter from Dr. Joel Hochman, who was the psychiatrist the prosecution used against me at my trial. He wrote, "I have never commented on your case, as I was not happy with the media circus that has always exploited it. I have been particularly unhappy with Mr. Bugliosi's distorted use of my professional testimony - to argue against your release. I testified that anyone's children could have ended up in your situation as part of a shared psychosis. He has repeatedly stated that I said just the opposite..."

It was a nice piece of validation, although completely unexpected. I hadn't thought of him in almost forty years and I was surprised he felt he had to write me. And the thing that seemed to upset him - what appeared to be his impetus for writing - was the way this case was and continues to be twisted for the commercial market. Perhaps he always had second thoughts about this case and after thirty-five years he felt he had to say something. Whatever the cause, it was a kind gesture.

Shortly after the publication of his book Vincent Bugliosi ran for Attorney General of California. If he had won he would have been a step away from the Governorship of California. And as Ronald Reagan had shown, that was a step away from a run at the White House. Bugliosi was beaten, ironically, by Ira Reiner who had been Leslie Van Houten's defense attorney. Mr. Bugliosi has gone on to become a successful author of true-crime novels.

Steven Kay, who was an assistant prosecutor at my trial and who represented the District Attorney's Office at most of my parole hearings, became a high ranking administrator in the Los Angeles DA's Office by the 1980s. I was told he always envied and resented the attention and money Vincent Bugliosi made off the Manson case. Then an investigation uncovered that Mr. Kay had made a deal to free Stephen Jesse Cisneros – a diagnosed sexual predator known as the "Riverbed Rapist" – in exchange for having him testify that a suspect in another crime had confessed while in jail. According to the investigation Kay admitted he felt there wasn't enough evidence to prove the other man guilty so in order to get the conviction Kay arranged to have Cisneros released in exchange for his sworn testimony. Following his release Cisneros kidnapped, assaulted, and/or raped ten women. When Cisneros was finally apprehended he admitted he'd lied in order to be released – no one had confessed to him.

When the deal that led Cisneros' release finally came to light Mr. Kay is reported to have dismissed the ten women who had been raped and assaulted as "just a small, teeny little offshoot."[270] According to the report Kay lost his high ranking administrative position.

I was told Steven Kay was subsequently moved to the LA DA's Compton department, far from the high profile cases he was used to prosecuting in Los Angeles. Which is why he missed prosecuting the O.J. Simpson case. And why he also missed the multi-million dollar book deal Marsha Clark received even after losing the case.

Following my conviction, civil wrongful death lawsuits were filed against me and my co-defendants as well as Linda Kasabian. The jury determined all of us, including Linda Kasabian, were equally responsible for the deaths of Steven Parent, Jay Sebring, Voytek Frykowski, Abigail Folger and Sharon Tate.

While I was on death row my son was legally taken from me because no one in my family was willing to raise him. His name and identity have been changed and sealed, so I have no idea where he is or how he is doing. I have since been told his name was changed to Paul, and whether or not that is true I like it. In the 1970's I watched a talk-show which featured a woman who handled difficult child adoption cases

---

[270] *"Deals Won Jail Informant Freedom to Attack Again,"* by Ted Rohrlich, Los Angeles Times

who claimed to have handled the adoption of one of the "Manson family children." Since my son was the only child who was taken away, it would have had to have been him.

My continuing separation from my son, even after all these years, remains the most poignant and enduring loss.

Obviously I wasn't executed.

Due to the convictions of a bare majority of the Justices of the U.S. Supreme Court, the death penalty in America as it was imposed up until 1972 was determined to be unconstitutionally arbitrary. The California Supreme Court invalidated the death penalty in California even before the U.S. Supreme Court could, determining it violated the California Constitutional's prohibition against unusual punishments.

My sentence was commuted to the harshest constitutional sentence California had at the time – seven-years-to-life with the possibility of parole.

Of the seven women on death row in California at the time the Supreme Court invalidated the death penalty, only me and my two co-defendants are still in prison. One of the other women was paroled after about eight years, the others were paroled in the early 1980's after serving about 13 years. None of these women ever came back to prison.

Life After Death

In 1974 I made the best decision of my life when I accepted Jesus as my Savior and Lord. Since that day my life has got better each and every year. I have been blessed over and over again. Charles Manson ceased being a part of my life in 1972, and this case stopped being a part of my life in 1974. While I still take responsibility for my part, I no longer allow it to dictate what I am going to do in the future.

No matter what mistakes you may have made in the past, they do not give you any excuses for failing to move forward with your life to make the most of it and to be the best possible influence on those around you.

As for my co-defendants, I've never interacted with them much. A lot of that probably was residual resentment for my getting them indicted. It probably also has to do with their disinterest, as well as my own, in being associated with the past. I know they both have exemplary post-conviction records and both are regularly denied parole for little or no reason other than the crime.

Leslie Van Houten, after having her conviction overturned by the Appellate Court in 1976, was retried a second time. The State dropped the charges against her in regard to the Cielo Dr. crimes and only tried to convict her for the LaBianca crimes. The jury didn't convict her and so they tried her a third time. During the third trial the Court allowed her bail and she spent nine months out of prison, living in Southern California and driving back and forth to work every day and no one even noticed.

At her third trial, instead of trying her for murder the State tried her for felony-murder, which means they claimed she merely intended to rob Ms. LaBianca and had no idea anyone was going to be harmed. Because that's a felony in itself, if convicted she would be held culpable for the murders even though she didn't know they were going to happen and didn't participate.

She was convicted of felony murder and sent back to prison in 1978.

About twenty-five years after my conviction I was in a child development education class and my codefendant Leslie Van Houten happened to be in the class as well. I'd been interacting in class and talking about how I'd been kept away from my son during his early development and how much I resented that. During the break Leslie came up to me and apologized. She told me for over twenty years she'd disliked me because way back when we were all living at Spahn Ranch, Manson told her my son was being kept with the other children because I didn't want him. Since Leslie and I didn't interact back then she had no way of knowing it wasn't true.

Just another indication of the subtle ways in which Manson was able to instigate resentment and ill-feelings between people simply in order to make them easier to control.

In the end, as decades and decades go by, I've been able to see the work both of my codefendants have done in this institution, contributing to various community services and victim's services. And so now, even though I still do not interact with them, I can appreciate how much they've made of their lives in this constricting environment.

In the 1990's Patricia Krenwinkel gave the only interview I believe she's ever given. I was surprised to hear the one thing she felt she needed to stress over and over again was that there was nothing cool about what happened during our crime. Apparently she, like me, has received abundant letters from people interested with the crime and convinced it was something other than a horrible, senseless tragedy.

My hope for this book has from the start been that it will lay the crimes out in a way that makes them look like what they really were. There is nothing mystic about them. Nothing impressive. Nothing worthy of admiration.

It is also my hope something good will come out of this. Every year I receive dozens of letters from people asking me for advice in reaching their sons or daughters or their younger relatives concerning either drugs or the pitfalls of cults and gang-mentality.

Sometimes I get letters from police officers or correctional officers working with youth asking how to reach children and young adults when they get to the point where they're so alienated they no longer listen or trust anyone. And that's a tough question.

One of the most important things to take from this whole story is that actions lead to consequences. Freedom involves responsibilities. Freedom is a gift and a treasure. That's what I'd like to think young people will take from this story.

This is the past I have to live with, and I have to live with it every day. Unlike the reader, or the people who seem to think Charles Manson was cool, I can't think about it for an hour or so and then go on with my life. This is with me every day. I have to wake up every day with this and no matter what I do for the rest of my life and no matter how much I give back to the community I will never be able to replace what my crime took away. And that's not "neat," and that's not "cool."

And I want to apologize, once again, to the families of the victims. I want to apologize for what my actions, and my lack of courage, took from them. For the loss they've suffered, and which they continue to suffer.

Made in the USA
Lexington, KY
12 July 2013